Praise

"When your structure works, confidence follows. *The One-Page Keynote* gives experts a clear system for designing talks that resonate, persuade, and stick, without relying on charisma or theatrics. If you want your message to land with clarity and impact, read this book."

— **Dr Shadé Zahrai**, bestselling author of *Big Trust*

"Start with this one. The best book you'll find on making your keynote matter."

— **Seth Godin**, bestselling author of *This Is Marketing*

"As a co-founder of Talkadot, I'm obsessed with one question and one outcome for speakers: Did your message land, and did it move people to action? *The One-Page Keynote* is the clearest blueprint I've seen for building a keynote speech that earns attention, answers what the audience is already thinking, and drives real action, even if you're not a 'natural' on stage."

— **Arel Moodie**, Co-Founder, Talkadot

"Finally! A book that treats a keynote as what it really is: a designed experience that changes how people see something. *The One-Page Keynote* offers a smart, no-nonsense framework to shape the story, the argument, and the ask, without depending on charisma or theatrics. If you need to speak to 'sell' ideas, you need this book—now."

— **Tamsen Webster**, Founder, The Message Design Institute; award-winning author of *Say What They Can't Unhear*

"As someone who has spent decades helping executives, experts, and leaders transform ideas into influence, I am always interested when a book promises clarity over charisma. *The One-Page Keynote* delivers precisely that, and it does so with intelligence, humility, and practical rigor. If you are an expert who wants your ideas to be remembered and to create change, *The One-Page Keynote* deserves a place on your desk, not just your bookshelf."

— **Patricia Fripp**, CSP, CPAE, past President, National Speakers Association; author of *Deliver Unforgettable Presentations*

"Brian Miller knows first-hand that public speaking isn't magic—because he knows magic isn't magic. But he also knows that communication can do magic. And he understands—better than most rhetoric experts—how to make that happen. In this book, he teaches you the process, step by surprisingly simple step."

— **David Murray**, Executive Director, Professional Speechwriters Association

"*The One-Page Keynote* framework is for people like me—introverts who want to serve but keep getting asked to do it from a stage. This book makes it easier to say 'yes.'"

— **Chris Do**, Founder and CEO, The Futur

"For almost two decades, I've been asked, 'What's the best book about giving a great speech?' I've read many and honestly couldn't recommend any of them—until now."

— **Jon Yeo**, CSP, Curator, TEDxMelbourne

"Brian Miller does something rare in this book: He explains why great talks work without mystifying the process or attempting to turn speakers into performers they are not. The *One-Page Keynote* shows that what moves an audience is not charisma, clever stories, or stage tricks; it's structure. If you are an expert who already knows your material but feels like your message sometimes lands flat, this book will fix that. And if you are a strong performer who has relied on presence to carry your message, this book will make your work sharper, clearer, and far more effective. This is not about learning how to speak. It is about learning how to be understood."

— **Christopher Carter**, mentalist and keynote speaker; author of *In the Spotlight*

"This book makes positive influence feel accessible to anyone. Brian's OPK method walks you right up to total confidence, step by step. And he makes the important stuff unforgettable, with enlightening examples and personal stories that are both relatable and entertaining. Truly one of the most enjoyable business books I've ever read."

— **Sheperd Simmons**, Founder, Counterpart Communication Design

"Finally, keynote speaking made easy. This is the book I wish I'd had early in my corporate career. Back then, I had no idea that great speeches could be mapped out step by step. No more wondering what it means to 'step inside your audience's shoes.' Brian is the real deal. If you want to deliver a talk that transforms your audience, busts conventional wisdom or demonstrates why you're the expert, read this book."

— **Rebecca Okamoto**, Communication Consultant; Founder, Evoke Strategy Group

"*The One-Page Keynote* is by far the most useful non-fiction book I´ve ever read. All the principles are gathered in an easy-to-read format, and integrating them into my own speechwriting has led to a massive increase in engagement and impact. The real magic lies in the structure. From first-hand experience, I know *The One-Page Keynote* will dramatically improve your ability to reach the hearts and minds of your target audience."

— **Peder Tellefsdal**, PR Expert; Speaker; Author of *Rebranding the Church*

"Let's be honest: We've all sat through speeches and wondered if the speaker got lost on the way to their own point. *The One-Page Keynote* is a masterclass in creating talks with meaning, flow, and real impact. I'm a fan! And yes—I use it myself."

— **Martin Lespérance**, North American Inspirational Speaker of the Year 2024; author of *Inspire*

"This book got me with the first line: 'Most speeches suck.' Yes! That's because most speakers don't know, or refuse to accept, that a 'winning personality' isn't nearly enough. Listening is hard, and the way to beat that problem is structure—structure that comports with (even exploits) human nature. Brian's a magician, and in this book, he'll teach you one helluva trick."

— **Michael Long**, Instructor in Writing, Georgetown University; author of *Taming the Molecule of More*

The One-Page Keynote

How to design a speech that always works, no charisma required

Brian Miller

R^e^think

First published in Great Britain in 2026
by Rethink Press (www.rethinkpress.com)

For the experts whose ideas deserve to be understood by the people they're meant to serve.

A Note For Coaches And Consultants

This book is written for individual, personal use.

The One-Page Keynote™ structure described here is a proprietary methodology developed by Clarity Up. You are welcome to use it to design your own talks, keynotes, and presentations.

However, coaches, consultants, trainers, and facilitators may not teach, adapt, package, or apply this methodology with clients, teams, groups, or audiences as part of a paid or unpaid offering without explicit permission.

If you wish to teach, license, or use the One-Page Keynote framework in your professional work, including private coaching, consulting, speaking, workshops, facilitation, or training, you must obtain authorization.

Licensing inquiries should be directed to:
licensing@clarityupconsulting.com

Contents

Introduction: Design Beats Delivery Every Time

Most speeches suck. Even when they're delivered by smart, experienced, well-intentioned people—and especially when they're delivered by experts. Maybe that's what brought you here. Perhaps you've been asked to speak at an industry conference, your company's summit, a fundraiser, or a public event. You're honored, maybe even excited. But if you're being honest, you're also a little uncertain.

You know your subject matter, and there's no doubt you're the real deal. But deep down, you're wondering: *What exactly am I supposed to say? How do I hold their attention for thirty minutes? Do I tell stories, share my research, or both? How do I know if it's… working?*

Let's change that.

This is not a book about how to become a paid speaker. You don't need to crave the spotlight or build a speaking business to have a world-class keynote that you can deliver with confidence. That said, if you do want to get paid to speak, this book will absolutely help. Because what you'll learn here is how to design a speech worthy of professional fees. Like me, our clients may be paid $5,000 to $20,000 or more per speech.

But primarily, this is a book for experts—scientists, academics, researchers, credentialed professionals, and industry leaders—who are already being asked to speak (or are considering it), and who want to make those opportunities count. Whether it's on behalf of your organization, your field, or your big idea, you're here because you want to do more than sound smart. You want to create change. And a great speech can change everything.

The speech that changed my life

I'm walking across the dark, freezing parking lot of a banquet hall when my phone rings. It's 2015 and I've been a professional magician for nearly ten years, supporting my fiancé Lindsey through her master's degree and funding both of our lives with card tricks. In a few minutes, I'll be entertaining a room full of professionals in suits. But first, I have to answer the phone.

"Hi, this is Brian Miller."

"Yes, hi, Brian. I'm a local high school teacher, and I'm putting on a TEDx event in our community. We got your name from some folks who thought you might be a good fit for our event. Are you interested?"

Thus began my journey into public speaking. And public speaking anxiety.

I knew this was the opportunity of a lifetime, but every time I sat down at a blank page, I felt stuck. I had absolutely no idea how to put together a speech—what to talk about, how much, or in what order. I knew my subject inside and out, but I had no idea how to translate that into something valuable for a high school student, an engineer, a nurse, or whoever else might watch it on YouTube. I almost quit. My reputation was at stake, and backing out felt safer than bombing.

But that's not who I am.

I delivered the talk at TEDxManchesterHighSchool in June 2015.[1] When it hit YouTube a few weeks later, something unexpected happened: the views started climbing. Fast. 100,000 views. Then 500,000. Then a million and beyond.

Invitations flooded in—conferences, universities, massive corporations. Everyone wanted to know, could I do for them what I'd done in that fourteen-minute talk, but with a thirty to sixty-minute keynote instead?

Here's the thing: I had no idea what I'd done.

So I opened a blank page and tried to recreate the magic from scratch. I started delivering those speeches and the results were... fine. Attendees enjoyed them, organizers were pleased. But these talks weren't having the kind of impact my TEDx talk had. I knew something was off, that these speeches just weren't as good. I wasn't living up to my reputation or the organizers' expectations, based on the success of my viral talk. But I didn't know what was wrong or how to fix it.

And then I thought, maybe I'd accidentally stumbled into the right structure when I wrote my TEDx talk. I pulled out the outline and analyzed it. What made it work? What was different? I found a sequence. Specific beats that showed up in a specific order. A framework I hadn't realized I was following. So I tested it. I rebuilt my keynote using the same structure as my TEDx talk, and everything changed.

Within a few years I was the number one search result in the world for "human connection speaker," had spoken on hundreds of stages across five continents, and was one of the top-rated speakers at every event I attended.

I was the same speaker, but I had a different speech. And because of that, experts and leaders across the world began reaching out to me, asking if I could teach them how to give talks about their subjects that were as good as the talks I gave about mine. I said yes, having no idea if I could actually do it, and taught them the structure I'd been using.

It worked. It worked fabulously.

After their successful talks:

- A consultant quit their grueling day job and built their own values-based boutique firm
- A psychologist went viral and landed a follow-up book deal
- An advocate for survivors of child abuse spoke on panels around the world
- A PR expert secured speaking engagements on his passion topic
- A wealth manager received a standing ovation and their home city named a day after them (yes, really)
- A mental health advocate gained speaking representation
- A college student secured a prestigious fellowship
- An animal rights activist duo received multiple prestigious awards for social impact

Today I'm the founder and principal consultant at Clarity Up, a message design firm where we teach experts and leaders like you how to explain your big ideas to the people who need to hear them. And that structure I lucked into all those years ago is now a framework that we've taught to hundreds of individuals who have gone on to start movements, influence policymakers, get featured in prestigious publications, write books, and build companies.

The best part? You don't have to be a great speaker to give great speeches.

It's not you, it's your speech

When a speech doesn't land, speakers tend to assume that they are the problem. That they're not polished enough. They say "um" and "ah" too much. They don't gesture enough, or they gesture too much. They talk too fast, or too slow. Pace too much, speak in a monotone, are too frantic, or too rigid… But ideas don't get buried because the presenter isn't funny, smooth, or seamless enough. It's not the speaker.

It's the speech.

Sure, it's great to have both. Nothing brings me more joy than witnessing a brilliant speech delivered by a charismatic performer. But if you can only have one, choose a well-structured speech every time. Case in point: I brought a decade of experience as a professional magician into my speaking career. I was funny, engaging, charismatic, dynamic, interactive. And it still wasn't enough to overcome a mediocre speech.

Chris Anderson, head of TED, weighing up speaker versus speech, puts it this way:

> "They're both important. But if I had to choose, it's actually content. Because I will listen to somebody delivering really important or weighty information in a boring way. I'll stay with them. But if somebody is speaking nonsense brilliantly, it's just irritating."[2]

If you're starting a cult, focus on delivery. But if you're an expert trying to change the world by sharing ideas that matter... Design beats delivery every time.

Let's go make a dent in the universe

In this book you'll discover a repeatable framework for building a keynote speech from scratch. On any topic, for any audience, that always works—no charisma required.

In Part One you'll find out why the One-Page Keynote™ system works, get a top-level overview of what it is, and plan appropriately by narrowing in on your intended audience and topic. This is the foundational work that most speakers skip, and it will instantly put you ahead of the pack.

In Part Two you'll learn how to grab attention at the start of your speech. We'll conduct an audience analysis so we can meet them where they're at, define the overarching journey you wish to take them on, and create a one-sentence statement that serves as both your filter and your audience's North Star as you build and deliver the talk. This ensures that your audience puts away their phones and gives you a chance.

Part Three is where you'll learn how to earn engagement. Here you'll craft the opening of your speech by stating a premise, establishing the stakes, asking a powerful question, and qualifying why they should listen to you—you, specifically. This will guarantee that your audience is fully engaged and gives you the opportunity to make your case in the heavy, lengthy middle part of the talk.

In Part Four you will discover the difference between a typical speech's "main body" and how thought leaders present a compelling case for their ideas. You'll establish the typical ways people try to solve the problem your talk sets out to solve, shift how they see the problem, learn when and how to use data, choose from a variety of creative tools to support each point, and give the audience a specific action step to take following your speech. This way, your audience will actually consider your ideas and be more likely to put them into practice.

In Part Five you'll create forward momentum by painting a vivid picture of what's possible when your ideas are put into practice, and you'll learn how to end your speech with a punch. This ensures you never overstay your welcome, and the audience walks away buzzing about your ideas.

And finally, as a bonus, in Part Six I'll give you a handful of ways to add "magical" or unexpected touches to your speech, and a crash course on performance.

So that's where we're going. Let's begin the journey.

PART ONE
ORGANIZE YOUR CONTENT

When tasked with creating a presentation from scratch, most speakers begin in one of three places: slides, stories, or stats.

These are all bad ways to begin the speech design process because they are about what *you want to say*, rather than what the *audience needs to hear*. If you could design a great speech by thinking the way you normally think, and talking the way you normally talk, you wouldn't need this book.

What speakers need is a simple but detailed structure that is reverse engineered from the way humans actually take in and act on information. It's taken me ten years of professional speaking, hundreds of keynote engagements, and training hundreds more speakers to develop, hone, and master a system that does precisely this. I call it the One-Page Keynote™ (OPK) structure, and in this first part of the book focused on organizing your content, I'll set out the reasoning behind our system, reveal the structure, and explain how it works at a conceptual level.

1

The Eight Questions Every Audience Is Silently Asking

A great speech is not a series of interesting points. It is a sequence of interesting answers to questions the audience is already asking. If you know what these questions are, and the order they're asking them in, you can design your talk as a deliberate sequence of answers to those questions. The audience will then feel like you're in their head. Everything will feel seamless and, more importantly, fulfilling. Even mediocre presenters can deliver world-class speeches if they get this right.

So, what are those questions? Well, that depends on what type of speech you're giving.

Thought leaders

This book is focused on helping you build a particular type of speech: thought leadership-style speeches.

And yes, I also roll my eyes at that term. But just for a minute, forget about the term itself and all the self-proclaimed gurus abusing it on LinkedIn. What does it actually mean? When they speak, why do we view some people as thought leaders and not others, even where they are equally qualified (or in some cases even more so)?

We perceive thought leadership when an expert in a field reaches beyond their domain, connects their topic to an outside field or culture more broadly, and strongly, confidently recommends a course of action. By contrast, a speaker who stays within their domain and simply describes a phenomenon or field, is more likely to be considered an "expert." The table below summarizes the different kinds of speakers based on whether they describe or prescribe, and stay within or reach outside their professional or intellectual domain.

	DESCRIBES	PRESCRIBES
INSIDE DOMAIN	EXPERT	ADVISER
BEYOND DOMAIN	PUBLIC INTELLECTUAL	THOUGHT LEADER

Different types of speakers

Thought leadership is the type of speech you're going to learn how to give in this book. As such, I don't recommend the OPK structure for wedding toasts, investor pitches, government briefings, Monday morning all-hands meetings, or a State of the Union address. At least, not in its entirety. There are elements of this structure that will benefit other types of speeches, but that's an "off-label" use that I can't endorse without reviewing it personally.

Keynote speeches are a vehicle tailor made for thought leadership. And the structure you're going to learn in this book is tailor made for those kinds of speeches. I don't claim it's the only way to build a keynote. I don't even claim it's the best way. I only claim that it works—every time, for any topic, and any audience. It works because it answers the questions that attendees of keynote speeches ask themselves, in the order that they ask them.

The eight questions your speech must answer

These are the eight checkpoints your audience is running in their heads:

1. Should I pay attention?
2. Does this really matter?
3. Why should I listen to you?
4. Why can't I keep doing what I've been doing?
5. What's the solution, then?
6. How do I get started?
7. Is it really worth it?
8. What was this all about again?

If you do not answer these questions, if you do not give satisfying answers, or if you answer them out of order, your speech will not land as well as it could. Best case, they'll be entertained. Worst case, they'll be lost, bored, or confused.

So as you develop your speech you must occasionally stop and ask yourself, *What question is this part of my speech answering?* If you either can't identify that question, or it would make no sense for the audience to be asking it, reconsider your content.

This is how great speakers often give mediocre speeches: by shoving in all kinds of entertaining stories, amusing anecdotes, or interesting data and unexpected results… that don't answer a compelling or relevant question for the audience. When you align each part of your keynote with a specific question, you're designing a speech that meets the audience where they are, addresses their concerns, and keeps them engaged from start to finish.

Something that every keynote speaker must understand is that a speech is fundamentally different from a book. When we read a book we can pause, re-read sections, and take time to mull things over. If something doesn't click right away, we have the luxury of circling back. With a speech, your audience doesn't have that option. They hear each point exactly once and only in the order you present it. If you lose them at any point, there's no going back to explain it again.

This means your speech doesn't just need the *right ideas*—it needs the right ideas in the *right order*. Every section, each question, must build, logically and emotionally, on the one before it, guiding the audience step by step toward your big idea. When you get this right, the listener will feel like you're reading their mind—it's a magical experience.

Why go to the effort to give a great speech?

First, there are some practical concerns and the matter of pride. Perhaps you're worried about looking foolish. That's fair. You're an expert in your field, maybe even the world's leading expert on your topic. And now you're being asked to stand in front of a room and perform. What if you freeze? What if they don't laugh at your joke? What if you lose your train of thought, or say "um" forty-seven times, or forget to advance your slides? These are valid concerns. After all, your reputation is on the line. But there's something bigger at stake here: trust.

We're in a trust recession. Across industries and around the world, trust in experts is collapsing. According to Pew Research, only 23% of Americans express strong confidence in scientists.[3] Trust in educators has also plummeted.[4] And only one in three Americans believe "most people can be trusted."[5]

I don't entirely blame them. Because the smartest people doing the most important work have lost the ability to communicate about their ideas in a way that is clear, understandable, and relevant. Meanwhile, someone less qualified than you is explaining your field to the public. Not because they're more charismatic or funnier or better performers. But because they've figured out how to make complex ideas accessible—even if those ideas are oversimplified, misleading, or flat-out wrong.

Take Malcolm Gladwell. He's been criticized by academics for oversimplification, but he's clear. People can follow the argument when he speaks and discuss his ideas with others. That's down to structure, and it was there from the beginning of his work. Gladwell's charisma and charm came much later.

It's not that the Gladwells of the world are better speakers. It's that they've structured their message in a way people can follow and repeat, where true experts often bury the message under mountains of jargon and winding trails of unnecessary details.

What good is being smart if no one understands what the hell you're talking about? If people do not understand your ideas, they won't know how to talk about them. If people don't know *how* to talk about your ideas, they *won't* talk about your ideas. And if no one else talks about your ideas, your ideas die with you.

This is why you need to learn how to give great speeches. Not to compete with performers, but to make sure your legitimate expertise doesn't get drowned out by people who simply know how to package information better than you do.

Here's the good news: this is a learnable skill. You don't need to be funnier, more charismatic, or naturally entertaining. You don't need to overcome some deep-seated fear of public speaking or learn to command a room like a motivational guru. You just need to understand how audiences actually think, and structure your content to match. Structure doesn't confine you. It liberates you.

Summary

Where you are: You now understand the reasoning behind the system presented in this book. Each section of your speech's outline will answer a specific question that your audience is silently asking themselves. When you answer these questions in the right order, your speech will feel seamless and engage your audience.

What's next: In Chapter 2, you'll learn the One-Page Keynote structure itself—the same framework I accidentally discovered in 2015.

2

The One-Page Keynote Structure

Your job is to design a talk for how humans actually think, react, and engage. That's what the One-Page Keynote™ (OPK) structure does. It delivers a compelling answer to each of the eight questions audience members are silently asking themselves, and in the order they're naturally asking them. And because the order of ideas feels natural to listen to, many speakers find the OPK structure intuitive to work through, which has an unexpected bonus—it's easier to rehearse, memorize, and internalize.

The best part? Using this structure you can outline your entire keynote on a single typed page.

Here it is:

1. **Introduction**
   - **Premise:** Meet the audience where they're at
   - **Stakes:** Remind them what happens if they don't act
   - **Core Question:** Ask the question your talk answers
   - **The Story Hook:** Tell a story that qualifies you as a trustworthy guide
2. **Argument**
   - **Status Quo:** Explore the current solutions and why they fail
   - **Paradigm Shift:** Propose a new way of thinking
   - **Action Step:** Tell them the very first or next thing they should do
   - **Success:** Paint a picture of what becomes possible with this shift
3. **Conclusion**
   - **Core Message:** Deliver the main point
   - **Mic-Drop:** Leave them with a memorable, repeatable one-liner

The closer you can map your talk on to these elements, in this order, the more confident you can be that the talk will work. And by work, I mean move the audience to action.

Throughout this book you'll encounter many examples of talks we've worked on across a variety of fields and topics, from marine science to psychology to animal rights, to self-help and personal success. But you will also follow the development of a single (real) talk from start to finish, which will serve as our throughline example. That talk is about stress among high achievers, and was delivered by Erika Coleman at TEDxOneonta 2025.[6]

My team and I were building this talk with Erika during the same time I wrote this book, and at the time of writing, she has delivered it, though it is not public yet. But while waiting for the TEDx recording to hit YouTube, she has delivered a version of it many times to organizations, and it is rapidly becoming her signature speech.

I chose this as our primary example for three reasons. First, because it's a topic with a tremendous body of research behind it, full of complexity, nuance, and caveats—and it was our task to smooth out, simplify, and clarify all this to produce a short talk that could be delivered to a general audience. Second, because managing stress is a topic that benefits the kinds of people we tend to work with. Since you'll be spending a lot of time with this talk as an example, hopefully you will enjoy the content itself. And finally, because Erika is precisely the kind of person this book was written for. As such, it's important that you know who she is before we begin learning from her talk.

Meet Erika Coleman

"I'm a recovering overachiever."

Sitting across from me is a woman whose smile has overtaken her face. She's wearing a vibrant blue professional shirt and has unusual streaks of gray through her hair—an asset that, as a young woman, helped her appear older and thus able to command more respect from "suits." The first word that comes to mind? Studious. And it turns out, I'm not far off.

Erika holds a master's in organizational psychology from Harvard, where she studied stress and wellbeing. In her previous life she was the founder and CEO of a seven-figure virtual training company, which taught organizations how to deliver successful webinars that people love attending. And now, as a "recovering overachiever" herself, she wants to share what she's learned—what she's still learning—about managing stress, in order to help others avoid some of the pitfalls she's faced and succeed on their own terms.

What might ordinarily be a self-help talk with an inspirational tone is strengthened by her business accomplishments and academic study. Where many speakers lean too motivational, Erika's Achilles' heel is her unadulterated love of science, research, and data.

Erika's One-Page Keynote outline

Let's begin by looking at Erika's entire talk mapped onto the OPK structure:

Introduction

Premise: We all want to be seen as competent and capable, but in an effort to achieve success we tend to overwork, which can lead to exhaustion.

Stakes: Almost half of US workers feel burned out or close to it.

Core Question: Can we reduce stress without sacrificing success?

The Story Hook: "My mom was my champion who supported everything I did, including building my values-driven business. But then she got sick, and at the same time my business was struggling for the first time.

"I worked harder and longer to help my mom and save my business, but in the end, I lost both: my champion and my purpose. For a while, I couldn't get back up.

"Eventually I went to Harvard to study stress and wellbeing, where I learned how high achievers can reduce stress without sacrificing success, and now I share that with everyone who will listen."

Argument

Status Quo: When we are stressed out, people tend to give us advice that falls into one of two categories:

- Do less (take a break, go on vacation, delegate)—but this doesn't work because to high achievers it feels like "care less," which they don't accept.
- Do more (time management, yoga, exercise, drink water, see a therapist)—while all of these can work, the effort often feels overwhelming, and can push someone on the verge of burnout over the edge.

Paradigm Shift: You can give your best without giving your all. Overachieving does not mean overextending. "Leaving it all on the court" only works if it's the last game you'll ever play. Instead of overachieving or under-achieving, we can learn the art of "even-achieving."

Action Step: Two questions to help you even-achieve:

1. Individual health: Ask yourself, *If I continue at this pace, when I'm done, will I have enough energy left to celebrate?*
2. Social health: Ask a loved one, "In the last month, have I been present enough for you?"

Success: When you even-achieve you can get everything done that needs to be done without sacrificing your ability to continue doing your best tomorrow.

Conclusion

Core Message: We don't have to give our all to give our best.

Mic-Drop: Everyone deserves the chance to reach for success without drowning in stress… and that's the art of even-achieving.

This sparse bullet-point outline fits neatly on a single typed A4 page. And Erika could, if she needed to, deliver the talk from this alone (and she has).

So, that's the OPK structure. It's what you'll be working from and toward throughout the course of this book.

An important note: do not try to script your entire keynote, word-for-word. Instead, bullet point your ideas at a high level. Just put enough on the page to jog your memory of the content of that section.

Later, in Chapters 18 and 19, we'll refine and enhance your main points with creative tools. Then, in Chapter 23 you'll discover a handful of advanced techniques that add a touch of magic to your talk, and in Chapter 24 I'll teach you a few simple ways to really bring it to life on stage. Trying to write a full script too soon is the fastest way to get stuck. Right now, your only job is to outline it. We'll fill in, shape and strengthen it later.

Visit https://clarityupconsulting.com/opk to access a companion resource hub with a blank One-Page Keynote™ Workbook, plus additional sample speeches laid out in the OPK format.

Summary

Where you are: You've seen the full One-Page Keynote structure and Erika's example. You understand that your speech has three major parts:

1. Introduction (Premise, Stakes, Core Question, Story Hook)
2. Argument (Status Quo, Paradigm Shift, Action Step, Success)
3. Conclusion (Core Message, Mic-Drop)

What's next: Before you can answer your audience's questions or begin filling in your keynote outline, you need to know who you're speaking to and what you're talking about. So let's figure that out.

3

Choose Your Audience And Topic

I'm at the airport ignoring the gate agent's instructions to stay seated until my boarding group has been called, when I hear a high-pitched shriek. It's a four-year-old girl sprinting down a moving sidewalk like Wonder Woman, laughing hysterically while her mom frantically chases after her. When her mom finally catches her, they ride together until the sidewalk stops, and then her mom scoops her up, turns around completely, and walks all the way back past me to get to their gate—which was in the complete opposite direction the girl was running. While it makes sense to a toddler, for us adults there's no sense moving fast if you're heading in the wrong direction. And there's no point writing a talk if you don't know where it's going.

So, where is your talk going? What journey are you taking the audience on?

Whether you're building a talk proactively, in case you're ever given the opportunity to speak, or you've already been invited to speak by an event organizer who wants you to talk about something specific, these are critical questions. There are too many possible points, stories, facts, and angles to cover everything—you'll have to focus.

For example, I'm often invited to speak about human connection. Great, but what about it specifically? I could talk about empathy, understanding, cross-cultural communication, interdepartmental communication, leadership, introverts versus extroverts, personal relationships, professional relationships, listening skills, speaking skills, talking to strangers, networking, remembering names, asking questions, making small talk, values and beliefs… Can you see the problem?

Experts often can't decide—or refuse to—and end up trying to cover a little bit of everything, which results in a speech that's confusing and exhausting. So before you work through the OPK structure, you need to answer some key questions.

Who is the audience?

You're never speaking in a vacuum, and you're never speaking to yourself. In an interview with me about how to get people to listen to you, Julian Treasure, five-time TED speaker and communication expert, explained:

> "Communication is not linear—it's circular. How I speak affects the way you listen. How you listen affects the way I speak. How I listen affects the way you speak. How you speak affects the way I listen. Round and round all the time."[7]

When we think about having a conversation, that makes sense, right? The person is right in front of you. You know you're speaking with someone specific. But it's easy to forget that the same is true when speaking from a stage or in front of a room. There's no such thing as an audience, really. It's just a group of individual listeners all bunched together. And like individuals, audiences have personalities, whims, interests, and preferences.

As professional communicators we must always remember that there is someone on the receiving end of our communication. The speech you design is for them, not for you. So, who are they? Are they nurses? Accountants? Mid-career professionals? Attorneys? High school students? University administrators? Government employees? Senior political leaders?

If you've already been asked to speak at an event, you know the answer—and if you don't, immediately ask your event organizer. (You can watch a video training on how to run a pre-event call via the resource hub at the end of this chapter.)

But if you are building a speech in anticipation of pursuing speaking engagements, you get to choose. Here are some prompts to get you started:

- Who are you most passionate about helping?
- Who would get the most value from learning what you know?
- Who would find your insights most enlightening or transformative?

These are very different questions and, as such, you'll probably end up with very different answers.

If I were to answer them, as a speaker on human connection, it would be something like this:

- Who am I most passionate about helping? Professionals in helping fields (i.e., nurses, counselors, social workers, etc.).
- Who would get the most value from learning what I know? Salespeople.
- Who would find my insights most enlightening or transformative? Students and young professionals.

In my career, I've spoken to all three of these groups. And depending on who I'm in front of, my presentation alters slightly. You'll see why in Part Two when we do an audience analysis. But for now, how do you choose which audience to write your speech for?

At this moment, go with your gut. Choose the audience that feels right. And if they all seem equally good, flip a coin. A three-sided coin, apparently. You're not marrying this choice. You're picking a starting point so you can actually build something.

Erika Coleman, who you met in the previous chapter, chose "high-achieving professionals" early in our journey, and it stuck. But she just as easily could have chosen "working moms" or "honors students," which would have led us down a different path.

Choose your audience, for now.

What's the angle?

Okay, so you've chosen an audience (or your event planner gave you one), and you know the topic you'll be speaking about (because either you've been asked to, or it's whatever you're an expert on). Think of your topic as your general domain. But as I mentioned, topics are broad. I gave you my example of human connection, but it's also true of financial planning, artificial intelligence, waste management, biomedical science, metaphysics, gut health, etc.

You'll need to pick an angle in order to move through the OPK system. What do I mean by an angle? An angle is a sub-discipline or a particular lens through which you see that topic.

Let's say I'm working on a speech on human connection, and the audience is college students. In that case, the angle I choose is "talking to strangers." It has high value, both for the students listening and the organizers who booked me, hoping I can get them out of their dorms and interacting with others in the campus community and beyond.

But when I am speaking on this topic with an audience of professionals in helping fields, like nurses, the angle I choose is "understanding different perspectives." Again, because it's useful to them in their jobs (and in their life), and the folks who booked me will benefit from having nurses who are good at understanding their patients, and each other.

Erika had a much harder time with this question. She'd studied stress and wellbeing while doing her master's, but again, that's super broad. In an ideation session, Erika came upon the term "even-achieving," which we all loved. But what exactly does it mean? Erika graciously sent me her personal notes from our early work with permission to share them in this book. This is what she wrote about this phase:

> "A talk on 'how to be an even-achiever' would likely focus on the concept of finding balance

> and consistency in achieving goals, moving away from the pressure of overachieving and instead emphasizing steady progress, self-care, and a holistic approach to personal development across different life areas, rather than solely focusing on excelling in one specific domain."

That's five or six different possible talks (or workshops, or dissertations). We knew she couldn't give a useful talk covering all that ground, so we pushed her to choose an angle. Ultimately, Erika committed to "balancing stress with success" to start with. She has since built a handful of presentations, each with a different angle, in order to serve different audiences and events. But this early decision gave us the direction we needed to create the first version of it, which is what she ended up delivering at TEDxOneonta.

Now it's your turn.

YOUR TASK

Here are some prompts to get you generating angles:

- What's a common misconception about your work or industry?
- What do you wish people understood about what you do?
- What's a lesson you learned the hard way that you wish everyone could learn?
- What's something you can't stop thinking about, even when you're not at work?

Jot down your answers and then decide on an angle that matches your chosen (or given) audience.

Before you move on, complete these two sentences:

- My audience is...
- My angle on the topic is...

For example, Erika's audience is high-achieving professionals, and her angle is how to balance stress with success.

Now do yours. That gives us something to work with.

Visit https://clarityupconsulting.com/opk to access a companion resource hub with worksheets, prompts, and links to supporting resources like podcast episodes and articles.

Summary

Where you are: You've chosen an audience and narrowed your topic to a specific angle. That gives you direction and, more importantly, guardrails as you build this talk from scratch.

What's next: Now that you know where you're headed, and where you're not, it's time to dive deeper into the minds of your chosen audience. Who are these people? What do they want? Struggle with? Fear? Believe? And how can we use this information to grab their attention the second you hit the stage?

PART TWO
GRAB ATTENTION

Most experts don't want attention. Oops, I said it. But they do want their *ideas* to get attention. Here's the problem: if you don't get attention first, your ideas never will. Ideas don't speak for themselves.

Experts, and even many industry leaders, are used to living in the shadows, quietly doing important work while louder, more outgoing, or more "interesting" people are out there getting people to pay attention. Or they hope that the work itself is interesting enough that people will pay attention, simply because of how important it is. That's where great ideas die: in the dusty halls of academia and beige boardrooms—in the shadows, buried in self-doubt and a misplaced sense of humility.

What if I told you that you can get people's attention without shouting, doing jump-kicks, trauma-dumping, or using click-bait shock-factor nonsense? And, more importantly, that you can get people's attention in a way that opens the door to deeper, more meaningful engagement?

In this part of the book, you'll discover how to grab your audience's attention immediately upon taking the stage, by answering the first audience question: *Should I pay attention to this?*

4

Meet The Audience Where They're At

A short woman stands up at the back of the room and, without waiting for a microphone, shouts this question at me: "How do I get my husband to let me remodel the kitchen?"

I've just wrapped a half-day workshop with a room of 200 county-level elected officials and asked what questions they have. But I was not prepared for this one.

"Can you tell me more about that?" I ask her.

Darla tells me the kitchen is old, the cabinets are falling apart, the counters are worn, and the appliances don't work as well as they used to. "But no matter how many times I ask," she continues, "and even though we could afford it, my husband says he doesn't want to spend the money to remodel the kitchen."

I pause. I'm thinking about the most delicate way to ask the question that needs to be asked. And then I just blurt it out.

"Does your husband cook?"

"No."

"Does he host?"

"No, he just sits in the living room with his friends while I prepare food and bring it to them."

"Does he clean?"

She bursts out laughing. "What do you think? No, of course not. I clean."

"So," I gear up. "He doesn't cook. He doesn't host. He doesn't clean. It sounds like he pretty much never uses the kitchen at all."

Her eyebrows go up as she anticipates what I'm about to say.

"Then why on *earth* would he want to spend tens of thousands of dollars remodeling the kitchen?"

The audience bursts into laughter. Especially the husbands.

"Well," she exclaims, "he should still want to. Because *I* want to, and I'm his wife."

Better to leave that comment alone.

The known want

People care about themselves. Your audience does not care about your topic as much as you do, if at all. And they're cynical. They've been burned before—they've sat through dozens of confusing, boring, or irrelevant presentations that wasted their time.

So when you get up on stage the first question on everyone's mind is, *Should I pay attention to this?* And you need them to answer quickly—yes!

We care about ourselves, and we pay for relevance with attention. If your talk is not immediately and obviously relevant to the audience, they will tune out (or worse, walk out). It's audience first, always. Most speakers and indeed communicators begin with the question, *What do I want to say?* They should instead be asking, *What does my audience need to hear?*

Before you put a single bullet point on your keynote outline, write a single word of your speech, or create a single slide, you must understand who you're speaking to—what they want, struggle with, believe, or fear. These are called psychographics. Like demographics, they identify a person or group of people. But where demographics identify people by superficial characteristics like age, gender, geographic location, or income, psychographics identify people by their internal states—the way they see the world, the way they wish the world was, how they see themselves, and how they see others. Once we sketch out our audience's psychographics we can start creating the speech, building up from who we're speaking to instead of working down from our idea.

At this point, we're looking for our premise. A premise is something the audience already holds true without needing proof, justification, or otherwise convincing. It's the foundation of your talk. So let's find yours.

Start with what they know they want

What does the audience know that they want? Not what you think they need, but what do they already *know* that they *want*?

The simplest way to figure this out is the "Search Test." What is their desire, goal, or wish—something that they would actually Google? Imagine your listener sitting alone in bed at 2 a.m., staring into the sterile glow of their smartphone and typing something into the search bar.

This is where so many speakers, and indeed marketers and communicators more broadly, go wrong. I refer to this as the "discover your inner goddess" mistake. For a while in the 2010s there was an explosion of self-anointed life coaches on Instagram, all using language like "discover your inner goddess." It's cute, I get it. But ain't no one ever typed, "how do I discover my inner goddess?" into the search bar. Right?

So, what *do* people type? They might search, "how do I get my boss to notice my ideas?" or "how do I feel more confident when I look in the mirror?" or "how do I get people to stop interrupting me?"—you get the idea.

If they wouldn't type it into a search bar, they don't *know* they want it.

Erika discovers her audience's known want

Back in Chapter 2 you met Erika and looked at her OPK talk structure. When I first met Erika, she was in the same place you are: swimming around the open water of a blank page, searching for somewhere to drop an anchor. In our quest to find her premise, we had a conversation that went something like this:

"Erika, you're building a talk for high achievers. What is your speech about?"

"Oh, boy. That's a great question," she laughed. "Being happy? Thriving? Finding balance?"

"Okay, we're circling an idea. What does your audience want?"

"They want," she pauses, "a life of abundance."

I smile.

"Too vague, right?" She laughs again.

She's right, it's too vague. Because nobody searches, "how do I live a life of abundance?" Well, that's probably not true. I'm sure somebody has. But not the kind of people Erika is trying to reach.

"That's okay, what do you mean by a 'life of abundance'?"

"They want to thrive. They're burned out—ugh, I hate that term. But yeah, they're burned out."

"Why are they burned out?"

"Because they're high achievers, so they're trying to do everything at the highest level all the way, please everyone and never let anyone down."

Ah, there it is.

"So," I said, "it sounds like what they really want is to be competent and capable."

"Yes!" Erika shrieked.

"Okay, now a qualifying question: do they want to *be* competent and capable, or be *seen as* competent and capable? Because those are not the same thing."

She looked up and exhaled.

"Seen as. They want to be *seen as* competent and capable."

There we had it. Erika wrote down her audience's known want: "We want to be seen as competent and capable."

And indeed, if you Google it, there are dozens of pages of articles and posts about how to be seen as competent, and likewise capable, in professional environments.

YOUR TASK

Identify your audience's known want—the thing they would actually type into a search bar, AI chatbot or similar at 2 a.m.

To do this, think about:

- What questions would they ask Google, AI, or whatever futuristic robot we use to look up stuff? Start with "how to..." or "how do I..."

- Is this something they *know* they want, or merely something you think they need?
- If you said it out loud, would they nod and say, "Yes, that's exactly what I want"?

When you have it, write it down as a simple statement: "My audience knows that they want..." This is the first component of your Premise, and you can add it to your OPK outline.

Visit https://clarityupconsulting.com/opk to access a companion resource hub with worksheets, prompts, and links to supporting resources like podcast episodes and articles, including hub with a worksheet on finding your audience's known want, and a list of famous fictional characters' known wants, often delivered in song.

Summary

Where you are: You've identified what your audience already knows they want—the desire that's living in their heads, whether they've articulated it or not.

What's in your outline: You now have the first part of your Premise filled in for your OPK outline—your audience's known want.

What's next: Understanding what your audience wants is only half the equation. In Chapter 5, we'll identify the problem—the obstacle standing in the way of them getting what they want. Together, want plus problem become the foundation of your Premise: the thing your audience already holds true before you say a single word.

5

Pinpoint The Source Of Their Struggle

So we've identified your audience's known want, as related to your topic. But since they haven't gotten this thing yet, something must be in their way. We're going to call this our "core problem."

The core problem

To arrive at your core problem, the question you need to ask yourself is, *Why is the audience struggling to get what they want?*

What are the obstacles in their way? We're looking to identify one issue to be the core problem for our Introduction.

External and internal problems

Problems tend to fall into one of two primary categories: external and internal. An external problem is something that exists in or relates to the world outside of us, i.e., "My boss won't let me," "I don't have enough money," "There's too much conflicting advice," "The mountain is too tall." By contrast, an internal problem stems from how we feel inside, i.e., "I'm not smart enough," "I'm overwhelmed," "I'm an imposter," "I'm not strong enough."

Just like the known want, the question here isn't what *you* think the problem is, it's what does *your audience* think the problem is?

Let's get back to Erika. She knows that the real problem for high achievers is a misunderstanding of what it means to give your best. But we can't go there, not yet—she'll make that point later during the Paradigm Shift. For now, she needs to articulate why high achievers *think* they're struggling to be seen as competent and capable. And that's pretty straightforward: high achievers think people don't notice their achievements. So they do more work, take on more projects, put in more hours. The more you do, the more exhausted you are, which intensifies the feelings of not being seen as competent and capable, which leads to working even harder and longer... and on and on, in a vicious cycle.

This is an *external* problem: *"No matter how hard I work, nobody notices my achievements."*

Had Erika identified an internal problem, it might have been something like: "I don't feel worthy of my success," or, "I'll never live up to expectations," which are also obstacles to feeling seen as capable and competent.

The biggest difference between external and internal problems is that external problems feel like someone else's fault, i.e., "It's just not fair!", "They're out to get me!", whereas internal problems are, by definition, personal, and thus feel like our own fault.

"No matter how hard I work, nobody notices my achievements" and "I don't feel worthy of success" are two sides of the same problem coin, but they feel very different. So which one should you be guided by? Choosing between an external and an internal problem is really about understanding how your audience is motivated. Are they more motivated to right a wrong in the world, or to "fix" themselves? In Erika's case, we went with an external problem to ease the transition into her talk, which, as you'll see, becomes increasingly personal and inward-focused.

Want + problem = Premise

You can now pair your audience's known want and the core problem or obstacle (internal or external) in their way to create a strong premise. Erika's Premise became: "We all want to be seen as competent and capable, but in an effort to achieve success we tend to overwork, which can lead to exhaustion."

Before you move on, though, use the Premise test. To test your Premise, consider: if those were the first words you said on stage to a room full of your ideal listeners, would at least 90% of the audience nod along as if to say, "Yes, that's right"? If so, you're golden.

Let's take a look at another example.

Meet Dr. Jacob Levenson

Judah Jacob "Jake" Levenson, Ph.D. is a marine biologist working on the next generation of animal telemetry, which is the science of tracking animal movement in order to protect the ocean, wildlife, and industries that are impacted by the ocean and its wildlife. These are things that matter deeply to scientists, but when I met Jake he was preparing to speak to a more general audience. We might describe his audience as "science enthusiasts," and his angle as "innovative animal telemetry science." Whew.

Even science enthusiasts don't sit around wishing we had better animal tracking technology, so what do non-scientists know that they want, that we could build his talk around? It's not obvious, and so Jake and I wrestled with this for some time. I was determined that his keynote would reach people in a way that few conservation or environmental talks do.

He began where most marine biologists would begin: we all want to protect the ocean. Except, that's not really true, is it? When was the last time you did something that suggests you care deeply about protecting the ocean? When was the last time you searched for ways to help ocean conservation efforts? Not as a fleeting thought or in the abstract, but because you really and truly wanted to take action? If we're honest, the answer is probably "rarely, if ever," for most of us.

I reminded Jake that he wouldn't be speaking to a room of his peers, or even to scientists. He'd be delivering a public-facing talk to people with a passing interest in "science stuff." But Jake is a scientist and, like most of us, stuck inside the perspective of his own field. He offered some more wants:

"We want to discover the unknown patterns of ocean wildlife."

Only marine scientists want this.

"We want energy security."

Maybe, if you're talking to politicians.

"We want to ensure the continued prosperity of humanity."

Closer, but too broad.

I asked him, "Jake, just answer this: what is your technology really good for? What does it help us do?"

"Well," he said, "it's helping us protect ocean features and creatures."

"And why do we want to protect the ocean features and creatures?"

"They're important to us for lots of reasons—food, air supply, the economy. If we lose them, we're in real trouble in a bunch of ways."

And there it was, hidden in plain sight. Something that every listener, even in a broad non-science audience, knows that they want. Did you catch it?

We all want to protect the things we care about.

So, that's the known want. Onto the core problem. Why might we struggle to protect the things we care about? What's the obstacle? I again began in Jake's world, searching for a bridge to his audience.

"Great. So help me understand, what makes protecting the ocean so tricky?"

Jake didn't hesitate, "The ocean is dynamic. It's always moving, always changing."

Bingo—our obstacle: some things are hard to protect because they're always moving. That's not specific to the ocean or the field of animal telemetry. It's something everybody holds true in different ways. That's what we want in a premise—something we don't have to make a case for.

If Jake built his talk up from "We need to create better animal telemetry technology" or even, "We need to protect the ocean," he'd lose almost everyone immediately. Like most scientists do. Instead, Jake's Premise became: "We all want to protect the things we care about. But some things are hard to protect because they're always moving." This was the springboard we needed to move the audience from something they already held to be true—the need to protect the things that matter to us—to the topic he wanted them to engage with: animal tracking technology.

How to convince your husband to let you remodel the kitchen

When Darla (our audience member from earlier) protested that her husband should care about remodeling their kitchen because she did, I had to laugh along with the audience. That is precisely the kind of wishful thinking that gets experts into trouble.

I said, "Okay, let's back up. Tell me about your husband."

"Well, he loves fishing. He's going to retire in a few years and he wants to buy a lake house so he can fish all the time."

"Oh. Will you be selling your house when the time comes?"

"Yes, to purchase the lake house," she confirmed.

"Darla, do you think it will be easier to sell your house, and possibly get more money for it, with a modern, recently remodeled kitchen?"

"Of course."

"Then start there."

Darla could build an argument up from what her husband wants, what he cares about, and what he is struggling with, to get him on board with what she was saying. If Darla were designing a speech to give to her husband, the premise would be: "You want a lake house when you retire, but we need to sell our house to have enough money to fund it."

You'll never convince someone who doesn't use the kitchen that they should make it prettier and easier to use. But Darla might convince her husband to invest in a project that will make it easier to get his lake house. And along the way, she gets a remodeled kitchen. Win-win.

YOUR TASK

In this task, you'll identify the known want and problem pair for your audience. You already have your known want; to get your core problem, follow these prompts:

- Think about your audience, why do *they* think they are struggling to get what they want? This is your core problem.
- Write down what you think is your audience's core problem, and create your premise statement: "We all want X, but unfortunately Y."
- Then, test it. If you said, "We all want X, but unfortunately Y..." would most of your audience be nodding along in silent agreement? If yes, you've nailed it—this is your Premise. Write it in your outline. If not, revisit.

Visit https://clarityupconsulting.com/opk to access a companion resource hub with worksheets, prompts, and links to supporting resources like podcast episodes and articles, plus a worksheet on finding your audience's primary problem or obstacle.

Summary

Where you are: You've identified your audience's known want and the core problem they perceive to be standing in their way. You can complete this sentence: "My audience wants [X], but they're struggling with [Y]."

What's in your outline: The Premise section of your OPK outline is now complete, comprising of a statement that combines your audience's known want and problem.

What's next: Known wants and problems define the external journey your audience is on. In Chapter 6, we'll dig deeper into the internal journey—the fears and beliefs driving their behavior. This becomes the emotional foundation of your talk.

6
Define The Change You Seek To Create

As well as an external journey, you'll also be taking your audience on an internal journey, which they may or may not be aware of and, more importantly, probably wouldn't admit out loud even if they are. Yet if you can offer internal transformation—that is, help them become a different kind of person as a result of your speech—you'll massively increase the likelihood that they pay attention.

Known wants and problems describe the external journey—what your audience is trying to accomplish in the world. By contrast, the internal journey is defined by fears and beliefs, and in this chapter, we're going to address both, in different ways and for different reasons. Let's begin with beliefs.

Beliefs

Beliefs are probably trickier than fears to nail down, because most people don't state their beliefs outright. When trying to identify your audience's beliefs, ask yourself, what are their deeply held, perhaps mistaken or misguided assumptions about the world?

I've been having back spasms since my early twenties. They happen once a year or so and are debilitating. Like, "I'm stuck on the couch and can't get up, yelling for my wife" debilitating. Like, "I can't play with my kid or sit at my desk to write an article" debilitating. When I get a back spasm, it's a total life pause. But with the combination of a heating pad, rest, gentle stretching, and over-the-counter meds, I'm functional again within a few days.

Every doctor has told me the same thing: to prevent back spasms, I need to strengthen my core. And yet, I've never done it. It's not a money thing. I have the money to do physical therapy, and even if money were a problem, there are tons of free exercises and videos I could follow. So, why aren't I taking care of this major issue? Because daily PT takes time that I do not have.

At least, that's what I believe. It's a belief so ingrained that no matter how many times people tell me about the long-term preventive solution, or how many testimonials I hear from people who it's worked for, I can't get myself to do it.

"I'm a dad who runs a business. I don't have time for physical therapy."

Until someone helps me break that belief, or replaces it with a different one, I'll never sign up for your PT program or "fitness coaching for dads" service. Now, this belief is clearly unfounded. I know a lot of dads who run businesses and have more kids than I do, who also find time to work out or go to PT. But it feels true for me. For me, it's a deeply held preexisting assumption about the world.

Your audience holds beliefs like this. And no matter how big their problem or how good your solution, you won't get them to move an inch while these beliefs still stand.

How to discover people's beliefs

We can't deal with our audience's beliefs unless we know what they are. But it's tricky, because you can't just ask people. Most people wouldn't know how to answer the question, "What do you believe?" And yet they believe many things.

Here are some examples of beliefs:

- "I'm not a creative person."
- "I'm too old to learn about AI."
- "The world is a dangerous place."

- "Everything happens for a reason."
- "Nobody can do this job as well as me."
- "Money doesn't grow on trees."

If you pay close attention, you'll notice that most people include the following words and phrases when describing their deep-seated beliefs:

- Always / never
- Everyone / no one
- Should / shouldn't
- Can't
- Deserve
- "I'm not the kind..."
- "There's no way..."
- "If only we..."

Additionally, watch out for emotional responses, particularly those that seem out of proportion to the situation. That's a clue that there's an underlying, unspoken belief at play.

Beliefs form the foundation of your Paradigm Shift, which you'll learn about in Chapter 15. For now, see if you can jot down a handful of beliefs that your audience likely holds; beliefs that would prevent them from going on the journey with you, or taking action on your big idea. Then choose the one most likely to prevent them from taking action and label it their "core belief."

For Erika, there was a huge lightbulb moment when we uncovered her audience's relevant core belief: "In order to be successful, I must give my all."

Now, onto a slightly easier topic: fears.

Fears

This is about what's keeping your audience up at night. I'm talking about sweating, shaking, can't fall asleep. Fears are the things your audience is truly worried about, deep down.

If you're a business owner, you should be able to answer this question about your customers. And if your customers are your audience, then you're in great shape.

But if you're a more traditional expert—an academic, researcher, scientist, etc.—who isn't in sales or running a business, you may not have any idea what your audience is afraid of. Put yourself into their shoes, imagining what they want and what they're struggling with, and then jot down the first few potential "fears" that come to mind. Then ask yourself, *Is that really what they're afraid of?* You might need to think a few levels deeper to find what you're looking for.

Here are some prompts to help you discover your audience's fears:

- What's something this audience would only tell their therapist or best friend?
- What's an embarrassing mistake this audience would be terrified of making?
- What is this audience currently doing, or avoiding, because they're afraid of the consequences?

Erika found fears easier to identify than beliefs. As a recovering overachiever herself, she rattled off many audience fears including being mediocre, stalling, or even moving backward in their career. But deepest of all, high achievers fear letting people down—even (or especially) themselves.

Humans are motivated to avoid things they're deeply afraid of, and so fears often become barriers to your audience taking action. You'll learn about how to leverage those fears for your audience's benefit in Chapter 10 on establishing the stakes, and again in Chapter 21 on painting a vivid picture of success.

For now, jot down a few of your audience's likely deep fears. Then choose the one most likely to stop them in their tracks, and label it their "primary fear."

We then need to identify what the opposite of this primary fear is. When we know what your audience fears, and what the opposite of that state is, we can craft an internal journey.

Let's return to our examples. If Erika's audience is worried about letting people down, what are they feeling? They are feeling insecure. Thus, in order to bring about an internal or emotional transformation, by the end of her talk they should feel a sense of security, safety, or comfort. Our marine biologist Dr. Levenson hoped his talk would ultimately reach stakeholders—the kind of folks who can support innovation in animal tracking technology. He identified their primary fear as unreliable technology, and thus crafted a listener journey toward confidence in the reliability of the new technology.

YOUR TASK

Determine the change you wish to trigger by identifying your audience's core belief and primary fear.

Your prompts:

- What belief needs to be replaced?[8]
- What fear needs to be assuaged?

Make a note of your audience's core belief—we'll need it in Chapter 15. Then use this framework to craft an internal audience journey: From [fear] to [safety].

Visit https://clarityupconsulting.com/opk to access a companion resource hub with worksheets, prompts, and links to supporting resources like podcast episodes and articles, including one I authored on discovering your audience's beliefs.

Summary

Where you are: You understand your audience's deeper motivations—what they're afraid of (fear) and what they assume to be true (belief). You've identified the internal transformation your talk promises to deliver.

What's in your outline: You don't need to add anything from this section to your OPK outline—yet. You'll use the core belief in Chapter 15 when you craft a Paradigm Shift, and the fear when you establish the Stakes in Chapter 10 and paint a picture of Success in Chapter 21.

What's next: Chapter 7 brings everything together. You'll distill your audience, the impact you're creating for them, and the action they need to take into one sentence: your filter. This becomes your North Star for every decision going forward.

7
The One-Sentence Filter

I'm an hour into the latest James Bond film. After analyzing an inscription etched into the bullet used by an assassin, Bond discovers who made the bullet and is making plans to track them down.

He meets a former colleague for lunch at a Parisian café. She has experience with this mysterious bullet-maker and may be able to help Bond track him down. But in a rare moment reminding us that Bond is human, he drips mustard on his beautiful gray suit.

So Bond takes the suit to a local dry cleaner for same day service. He waits until the suit is returned, but discovers it has shrunk. Bond is livid—this is his favorite suit! But the dry cleaner refuses to take responsibility and insists the suit was always like that. What else can Bond do? He takes the dry cleaner to small claims court where they spend the next thirty minutes of runtime arguing over the suit shrinkage. Finally, Bond is made whole when the local dry cleaner is forced to provide compensation, and he can finally return to his mission.

Wait—sorry. That never happened. But it would be super weird if it did, right?

The Filter Framework: How to avoid losing the plot

At some point during the speech creation process, everyone loses the plot. We either stuff the outline full of more points than we could possibly cover in the allotted time, stare at a bullet point wondering if it's worth saying at all, or get stuck altogether.

If even you are not sure what points need to be made and which can be dropped, which stories should be told and which are superfluous, which stats are useful and which are irrelevant—how can you possibly expect the audience to complete their journey with you?

The good news is that we can avoid all of that fluffing about by taking just a few minutes to create a filter statement. Your filter is a one-sentence statement that contains what your speech is about, who it's for, and why it matters.

Once you've got this sentence, you'll never lose the plot again. Here's how it works.

The Filter Framework

This is the same framework we use at the start of all private consulting engagements. From working on a keynote speech to developing a communication campaign for a statewide healthcare system, to developing a presentation for the leaders of a federal agency, it's the same every time.

It's the same framework we use with animal rights activists, famous attorneys, renowned academics, and unicorn tech founders. We use it to prepare speeches for local fundraisers, high-stakes industry events, and internal company briefings. Which is to say, do not dismiss what you're about to learn because of its simplicity. Yes, it is simple. That's why it works.

The Filter Framework: For [audience] to achieve [impact] by [action].[9]

Wait, wait. This feels familiar…

Yes, back in Chapter 3 we chose your audience and topic. What we uncovered then were the crude components of the filter statement we're about to create: who you're speaking to, the impact as a result of your talk, and how to get them there. But now it's time to refine and sharpen your focus.

How to define your audience

You've already got a sense of who the audience is, but now we need to dramatically simplify it for the sake of your filter. The goal is to sum up the audience with a modifier plus a label.

First, return to the broad label of the people you'll be speaking to from Chapter 3, i.e., parents, entrepreneurs, college students, leaders.

Then ask yourself, what mindset or state of being would make that group most likely to need your talk? Are these people busy, passionate, anxious, burned out? Refer back to the want, problem, belief, and fear you previously identified for clues to help you nail down an appropriate modifier.

Example audiences

Put your label and modifier together to get an audience that's both specific and versatile, such as:

- Busy parents
- Passionate entrepreneurs
- Anxious college students
- Burned-out leaders

In Erika's case, it was "exhausted high-achieving professionals." Two modifiers make it even more specific.

Once you know and have written down who your audience is, the next step is to identify the long-term result of taking action related to your talk, which we'll call "impact."

How to define your impact

This should be easy, because we have already identified your audience's known want and problem. Simply articulate one of these as a result—either they get what they really want or overcome what they're struggling with. Useful impacts are universal—things that basically everyone in your identified audience would be thrilled to achieve or gain.

Example impacts

- Ensure their children want to remain a part of their lives as adults
- Grow their business sustainably
- Become confident professionals and engaged community members

Erika's impact was "to reduce stress without sacrificing success." When you have yours, write it down. The final step is to express what they'd have to do in order to achieve that impact. This is the action they need to take.

How to define your action

What would someone in your audience have to do in order to get the result you've identified? Bonus points if it's unexpected, and extra bonus points if it's not something that everyone would want to do. We call this "useful friction." If it's something anyone would be thrilled to do, it's probably not very interesting (and perhaps so obvious that no one would bother doing it). By contrast, if the action feels like something people wouldn't typically want to do, but it's positioned as the thing they *must* do in order to get what they want? This creates friction. Momentum. Change.

Think about what you might tell someone, one to one, to help them get what they want, or overcome their primary obstacle. Say it in normal language, like you'd use with a friend over lunch, then zoom way out and turn it into a principle. Let's say your action step was, "Call one person from your past and thank them for something." You could principle-ize that as, "Practice active gratitude."

Example action principles

- Prioritize connection over convenience
- Identify your deepest values

- Get comfortable being uncomfortable

For Erika, this was straightforward, because it's her proprietary solution. Her action step was "learn the art of even-achieving." But what if your talk is about systems or culture, rather than individuals? Then you need to identify the systemic or cultural action that would need to occur.

Examples of systemic/cultural action principles

- Invest in revolutionary space technology
- Reset our expectations for generative AI
- Commission more research on sun exposure

Again, once you have your action, write it down.

YOUR TASK

Okay, now that you've identified at least one audience, impact, and action, you've got all the components. Put them together like this to create your filter statement:

For [audience] to achieve [impact] by [action].

You may need to nudge the words around to create a grammatically correct sentence, and you can get away without explicitly stating the audience if they're implied by the impact.

Visit https://clarityupconsulting.com/opk to access a companion resource hub with worksheets, prompts, and links to supporting resources like podcast episodes and articles, including a Zoom call recording where my lead consultant and I conduct live hot seats with speakers trying to build their filter statements.

Using your filter to build your keynote

The filter statement is for you, not the audience. As you craft your keynote you will have moments when you're unsure about what to include or exclude. This is when you return to your filter statement and ask yourself: *Does this story, fact, slide, example, joke, exercise, etc. immediately and obviously support my filter statement?* If the answer is no, you cut it.

For Erika, her filter statement came out as: "If you want to reduce stress without sacrificing success, learn the art of even-achieving."

Dr. Levenson's was: "By investing in and leveraging revolutionary space technology, marine scientists can reverse the devastating ocean damage that impacts our plates, playgrounds, and paychecks."

Think of your filter as the guardrail that keeps your talk focused and intentional. It ensures you're building your speech up from a foundation of clarity, not down from an idea. By sticking to your filter, you'll avoid the trap of creating a disjointed, confusing talk and instead deliver a keynote that feels cohesive.

Summary

Where you are: You've created your filter statement. This is the invisible thread that holds your entire speech together.

What's in your outline: While it's not part of the OPK outline itself, you can write your filter at the very top of your outline page. Every story, stat, joke, or tangent you consider adding will be tested against this filter. If it doesn't support this sentence, it won't be included.

What's next: Part Two is complete. You've done the essential prep work—structure, direction, audience analysis, and a filter. You can be confident that your talk will grab your audience's attention; now we need to earn their engagement, enough to carry the entire speech. Part Three tackles your Introduction, the most critical few minutes of your entire talk.

PART THREE
EARN ENGAGEMENT

I was once at a baseball game where a fan jumped out of the bleachers butt naked and sprinted across the field until he was tackled by security. That dude definitely got our attention. We gasped, we laughed… and then we went back to the game.

The truth is, it's not that hard to grab people's attention. What's hard is keeping it. And that's the job of your speech's Introduction: to earn their engagement after grabbing their attention, enough to carry twenty, thirty, or even sixty minutes of stage time. This means there's more weight on your Introduction than any other part of your talk, because it's when your audience decides whether they're going to commit.

If I only had an hour to design a speech from scratch before walking on stage, I'd spend ten minutes building the outline and fifty minutes writing and rehearsing the Introduction. As such, the following chapters will be longer and more in-depth than previous chapters. It matters that you get this right.

With that in mind, let's design the Introduction to your talk.

8
Classic Ways To Open A Talk

You've just taken the stage, opened your mouth, and started talking. What are the first words that come out?

There are three traditional recommendations for how to start a speech. You can:

1. Tell a story
2. Share a surprising statistic
3. Ask a question

It's hard to know which to use, and that's because these are tactics, not strategies. First you need to know what the strategy for your opening is, then you can identify the best tactic to deliver it.

Your strategy? Convey relevance immediately.

Remember, when you take the stage or begin your presentation, there's only one question the audience is asking themselves: *Should I pay attention to this?* In other words, *Is this relevant to me? Will this be worth my time?*

If you don't answer that question quickly, they're gone. At best, they'll zone out; at worst, they'll start answering emails right in front of you. So whether you choose a story, a statistic, a question, or some other approach not mentioned here, the only thing that matters is whether it quickly and clearly tells the audience, "Yes, this talk is relevant to you and will be worth your time. Put your phone down and focus."

Let's explore the three classic options.

Option 1: Tell a story

We all know how powerful stories are. Telling a story is one of the fastest and easiest ways to connect with others, as stories create empathy and are far more engaging than facts alone. In theory. But most people either tell stories that take way too long to get to the point, tell an interesting but irrelevant story, or tell the right story in a boring or unengaging way.

Imagine you're at a party and Gerald, your friend's cousin who you just met says, "Let me tell you a story." Check your body right now—are you excited? No, you're bracing for impact. *How long am I going to get trapped here? And where is the guacamole?*

Well, the Geralds of the world sometimes give speeches. So while a story can be a fast-track to empathy, it can just as easily tank your talk before it starts.

When used effectively, the story tactic has many strengths, among which are that it:

- Conveys emotion
- Sparks imagination
- Creates curiosity

On the flip side, weaknesses of a story include that:

- It takes time to tell
- It requires some performance craft
- The point can get buried beneath details

When to choose a story

Here are a few reasons you might want to open with a story:

- Your talk is built from or heavily relies on your personal story
- You have a technical or dry topic that could benefit from some humanity
- You have a common or well-worn topic that needs differentiating
- You are a particularly captivating storyteller (be honest)
- The story can be told in under two minutes

Example: Erika grounded her cold topic with a warm open

As previously mentioned, Erika is most at home when she's knee-deep in data, research, and academia. To counterbalance the academic foundation of her talk and establish a warm connection with the audience as quickly as possible, we suggested she open with a story. This is the story she used:

> "One time I was asked to describe my mom in one word, and I said, 'champion.'
>
> "And then I watched my four sisters' faces as we realized that all five of us, without talking to each other, had each chosen the exact same word. My mom, Cindy, was a champion. Literally, her sports trophies filled an entire room—give that woman a ball and a stick and

> she came home a winner. But more than that, my mom championed other people.
>
> "You see, a lot of my friends were young parents who wanted to work but couldn't do it full time. And, as many parents of young children know, it's hard to find work that's accommodating in that way. So I built a company where my friends could work, on their time and in their way… And my mom loved that.
>
> "But in March of 2022, my phone rang. 'Your mom's in the hospital.' She had terminal brain cancer and at most had eighteen months left to live.
>
> "At this same time, my business was facing trouble for the first time, and I was terrified I would let all my people down. So, I worked harder and longer hours. I gave more and more to my business, my employees, my friends, my family, and my mom.
>
> "Each day, I gave everything I had. But after just fourteen months, my mom passed. And two months later, I closed my business. I lost my champion, and my purpose.
>
> "And so I finally gave myself permission to sit down and rest. But then I couldn't get back up."

This is a great story to open a speech with. It's joyous. It's devastating. It's human. And most importantly, it establishes the premise of the talk all on its own: in an attempt to live up to every possible expectation at the highest level, high achievers tend to sacrifice themselves and burn out in the process.

We'll explore storytelling techniques more in Chapter 12 on finding your story hook, and again in Chapter 18 when we learn about different ways to creatively support the main points of your argument.

Option 2: Surprising statistic

Imagine if I opened a speech like this: "Human brains have approximately 86 billion neurons."

Is that shocking? Interesting? Surprising? Helpful at all? There's a good chance you don't have any context for that statistic. If you're not a neurobiologist, you likely don't know enough about the field to be thrilled, terrified, or even curious.

If you open with a statistic expecting the audience to be shocked or surprised, but instead they're just "meh," you're like an amateur comedian at a Tuesday night open mic who delivers a punchline to silence. Not recommended. Plus, it's incredibly easy to deceive with statistics, either intentionally or by accident. Audiences are smart, and they've got an automatic BS detector that will go off if they feel misled or like they're missing contextual information required to fully understand the stat.

This tactic does have some key strengths:

- It's hard data
- It can inspire shock and awe

The main weaknesses are that raw stats:

- Lack context
- Are easy to manipulate

When to choose a statistic

Here are a few situations when or reasons why you might want to open with a statistic:

- The statistic is self-explanatory.
- It provides hard evidence for the problem.
- It is credible but counterintuitive.

Example: I opened with a statistic

For many years in my keynote on human connection, I would walk on stage and start my speech with these words:

> "Eighty thousand. That's how many people you meet and interact with over the course of a lifetime. Which means over the course of your

> life, you meet an average of three new people every single day."

It was counterintuitive, a complete pattern-interrupt that instantly grabbed the audience's attention. They'd start thinking, *Is that true? That can't possibly be true.*

But then I'd continue:

> "If that feels impossible, it's because we're not really paying attention to how many people we interact with. Treating them as transactions instead of interactions. But think, really think, about how many people you've already met or interacted with today. I bet it's more than three."

Using a surprising statistic was a quick way to convey relevance while establishing the core problem addressed in my talk. Having said that, we tend not to have our clients open with a statistic. It's so rare to find a stat that is truly self-contained and also implies or states the premise of the talk in a way that's credible.

Option 3: Ask a question

Every trial attorney will tell you, "Never ask a question you don't know the answer to." In other words, if your case can turn on the answer to this question, and you don't know for sure how the witness will answer, it's not worth the risk of asking it.

Here are three types of questions speakers tend to gravitate toward opening with and why, if you're planning to open with a question like this, you might want to reconsider or at least be very careful.

Superficial questions

Speakers often use these types of questions without even realizing it. I call these "forced engagement" or superficial questions, and you know exactly what they are. It's questions like:

- "How's everybody doing today?"
- "Are you ready to learn?"
- "Isn't this a great event so far?"

These questions are intended to get the audience to whoop and holler, to cheer or applaud—for no damn reason. They carry no narrative, emotional, or intellectual weight.

Superficial questions are by far the least egregious of the bunch but are nonetheless annoying. Do not waste your audience's time or attention on these.

Leading questions

A leading question is a question that implies a specific answer. For example: "Don't you want to be healthy?"

There's only one answer to that question—nobody would truthfully answer "no"—which raises all kinds of silent alarm bells. As an audience member, that makes me suspicious of whatever you're going to say next. It feels like you're setting a trap.

Avoid leading questions early in the speech, and completely if you want (or need) your audience to trust you.

Rhetorical questions

A rhetorical question is a question that, by definition, is not meant to be answered. For example: "Is there anything more important than protecting the ocean?" This type of question *can* work—if you absolutely know for sure how your audience would answer it, and it supports your argument. Asking the above question in a room full of marine biologists? Great. But a general audience? They will immediately be able to think of things that are more important (to them) than protecting the ocean.

Avoid rhetorical questions if you are trying to earn engagement and you don't know how the audience would answer.

The strengths of opening with a question are that it:

- Sparks curiosity
- Personalizes the topic instantly

- Positions you as a guide

The weaknesses of this tactic include that it's:

- Easy to default to rhetorical/leading/superficial questions
- Risky if you don't know your audience's likely answer

When to choose a question

There are bad questions, as I've described above, but there are also great ones. Here are a few cases where you could open with a question:

- When the question creates genuine curiosity
- When the question inspires personal, private self-reflection
- When you want to frame the talk as a collaboration, not a lecture

Example: Dr. Carole Blueweiss opened with a question

Dr. Carole Blueweiss is an expert on balance, and delivered a talk to help people understand that they have more control over how they age than they might think they do.[10] When Carole hit the stage she took a bright pink sock out of her blazer pocket, held it up to the audience, and asked: "When you put on your socks in the morning, how do you do it?"

You're already thinking about it, trying to recall this morning—right? That's why it works. She continued:

> "Do you sit down? Do you lean against the wall for support? Or do you balance on one leg? Believe it or not, the answer to that question may determine if the last years of your life are the worst years of your life… or the best."

Here, a question (followed by a series of qualifying questions) set up the entire talk by immediately making it relevant to the audience's lives, in a very personal way, by inviting self-reflection. Everyone puts on socks, and now as the listener, I'm curious: *What does how I put on my socks have to do with my health as I get older?*

So if you choose to open with a question, be sure it sparks genuine curiosity. In Chapter 11 we'll discover precisely how to craft the right kind of question, and when to use it in your speech for maximum effect.

YOUR TASK

Choose an opening tactic for your introduction, and make a note of this in the Introduction section of your OPK.

There are, of course, more options than the three presented in this chapter. You can open with a metaphor, a demonstration, an interactive exercise (more on creative techniques like these in Chapter 19)—but no matter which tactic you choose, the only thing that matters is that your opening quickly and clearly conveys relevance to the audience.

This is more of a creative choice than an analytical one, so play around with ideas for each option and see what feels right to you, and for your audience.

And if none of these resonates with you, hang tight. In the next chapter we'll discuss a fallback strategy that *always* works, no matter how you feel or who your audience is.

Visit https://clarityupconsulting.com/opk to access a companion resource hub with worksheets, prompts, and links to supporting resources like podcast episodes and articles.

Summary

Where you are: You understand three classic opening tactics: stories create emotion, statistics provide shock value, and questions spark reflection. Each tactic has strengths and weaknesses, but all must convey relevance immediately.

What's in your outline: You may now have an opening tactic in the Introduction section, but don't worry if it's blank for now—you have one more, failsafe option.

What's next: These tactics are powerful, but they're not the only options. In fact, there's one approach that works every time, requires no creativity, and guarantees your audience immediately understands why they should care. In the next chapter, we'll explore the KISS method.

9

When In Doubt, Explicitly State The Premise

On the wall of my office, behind my chair and visible at all times while I'm on camera, is a large three-by-two-foot panel custom-printed with the following words: "Just say the thing."

Having it up there means I don't have to interrupt my client during a session when they're rambling or jargon-bombing me. I can simply turn my body slightly and gesture to the words that have become my mantra in communication. I even trademarked it as the official tagline of my company, Clarity Up.

Sometimes the simplest solutions truly are the best, but speakers often get so wrapped up in creative techniques that they forget that there's another option for opening any talk: Tell the audience the premise of the talk in normal words.

The KISS approach

Back in Chapter 5 we discovered that the premise of a talk can always be built on some version of, "We all want X, but unfortunately Y."

That was our way of defining the premise for ourselves, so we have a foundation on which to build the talk. But you can actually just say it out loud to the audience, and it will serve as a functional, if not terribly exciting, opening to your talk.

We call this the KISS opener: **K**eep **I**t **S**imple, **S**tupid.

If I wanted to use the KISS approach, I could take the stage and say: "We all want our ideas to spread, but two things have changed in the last ten years. First, there's been a dramatic decrease in trust. And second, there's been an insane increase in noise."

Not only *could* I say that, I have—in many keynotes and workshops on the topic of message clarity. Within seconds, the entire room understands precisely what my talk is about and how it's relevant to them. No need for stories, questions, statistics, metaphors, demonstrations… yet.

Let's look at one of my favorite examples of this approach in action, from our client Peder Tellefsdal and his now viral talk at TEDxArendal entitled, "How to seek forgiveness when relationships are on the line."[11]

Example: Peder Tellefsdal's viral talk on forgiveness

Peder Tellefsdal is a delightful Norwegian family man, whose talk was born from personal demons. His first draft was all story—but the stories were long and winding. None of them would "get to the point" in under two minutes. I was convinced that Peder needed to open by explicitly stating what the talk was about in order to grab people's attention and earn their engagement for the storytelling journey he was about to take them on. Here's where we landed:

> "None of us wants to hurt the people we love. However, we have a tendency to act against our best intentions."

Those were the first words out of his mouth upon taking the stage. In the span of ten seconds, Peder gave the audience everything they needed to engage. He identified their known want—not hurting the people we love—and the core problem—despite our best intentions, sometimes we hurt people we care about. Peder's talk went on to accumulate nearly two million views and launched his speaking career.

The pros and cons of being explicit

The KISS approach has a few terrific benefits that must be balanced against a couple of major potential downsides.

Strengths:

- Very quick
- No creativity required
- Instant relevance

Weaknesses:

- Can come across as dry or academic
- Risks feeling abrupt or cold*

So while KISS is my preferred approach on paper, it can take some performance coaching or at least a bit of rehearsal to effectively open the talk by explicitly stating the premise.

* A note from Ioana (Jo) Jongsma, a presence and performance coach who often supports our clients at Clarity Up: "This is where delivery can change the game. The same truth can feel confronting, or it can feel validating, depending on how it's said. When in doubt, open with warmth—in your eyes, voice, and body language."

When to choose the KISS approach

Here are a few reasons you might opt to explicitly state the premise to open your talk:

- Your stories all take too long to convey the known want or core problem.
- The audience doesn't have enough or the right context for your presentation.
- You have a dense or technical topic that would benefit from quick framing.

We almost always write the first version of an introduction using the KISS approach, and only upon having completed the entire keynote outline do we consider if there's a more creative approach that would make more sense. But—and this is crucial—whether you open by explicitly stating the premise or choose a more creative approach, it's almost always worth explicitly stating it *at some point* during the introduction. So if you open with a story, follow it by explicitly stating the premise. Same for a statistic, a question, a demonstration, a metaphor, or a bit of audience interaction. Do not leave it to chance that the audience understands the foundation of the talk. Everything is built up from here, so make sure they hear it.

Example: Dr. Levenson's "Fitbit" demonstration

In Jake's talk on the next generation of animal tracking technology, his opening was designed to shock and surprise the audience.

"Please welcome Dr. Jacob Levenson…"

As the audience applauded, Jake entered the stage holding a bright orange rectangular object with wires coming off of it, the size of a large flashlight. Before he even hit the center stage spotlight, Jake began speaking:

> "This is a Fitbit… for whales."

The audience smiled and leaned in with curiosity and excitement. Jake continued:

> "It's basically a smartwatch that records every flipper stroke, every movement. It's very expensive. Sometimes it takes a year in advance to purchase.
>
> "And we attach it to the whale with suction cups. Why? Because marine scientists have decided that this whale is worth protecting. And unless we know where it is, where it's going, and how it behaves, we can't protect it."

Okay, so we've got a creative opening that grabs people's attention. But how does he keep their engagement? By following that up by explicitly stating the Premise in the form of the known want:

> "Now, we decide to protect things all the time—buildings, works of art, landscapes, and animals. And we usually decide to protect something for one of three reasons: health, economy, and legacy."

He briefly explores each of those three reasons for protecting things, so the audience fully understands how "protecting things" is relevant to everyone in the room. And then he delivers the core problem:

> "Protecting things is usually straightforward. We put a fence around it, designate a landmark, or store a treasure behind glass. But the ocean doesn't work like that. It's not simple or easy to protect."

Jake could have simply opened the talk with, "We all want to protect the things we care about," and we did consider doing this. But one day on Zoom he went, "Check this out" and held up a giant orange explosive-looking device to his webcam.

"What the hell is that?" I asked.

He got excited.

"It's like a Fitbit for whales. It's how we track them when they're out of our view."

And I said, "Dude, you have to put that in the talk. In fact, I think you should open with it."

It worked gloriously. But after the initial attention-grabber, we still needed to make sure the audience bought into the substance of the talk, and so we layered the explicit Premise into the rest of the Introduction.

Side note: Jake had successfully defended his doctoral dissertation just weeks before stepping on stage at TEDxFoggyBottom,[12] using some of the same message design techniques you're learning in this book. And when the event host introduced him as "Dr. Jacob Levenson" it was the first time he'd heard anyone say those words out loud. You can see it on his face, just briefly, as he takes the stage. It's beautiful.

YOUR TASK

It's time to design your opening.

You've got a handful of creative tactics to choose from—story, statistic, or question.

If one feels right to you immediately, roll with that. But if not, use the KISS approach and simply write out the known want and core problem as the opening to your talk.

You can literally never go wrong if you explicitly and plainly state the Premise ("We all want X, but unfortunately Y"). Sure, it may come off a bit cold or academic, but it's guaranteed to instantly convey relevance, which is always worthwhile.

Whichever tactic you decide on, write it in your outline.

Visit https://clarityupconsulting.com/opk to access a companion resource hub with worksheets, prompts, and links to supporting resources like podcast episodes and articles.

Summary

Where you are: You've designed your opening. Whether you chose a story, statistic, question, or the KISS approach, you've answered the audience's first question: *Should I pay attention to this?* You've conveyed relevance immediately.

What's in your outline: Under "Introduction" in your OPK outline, you now have your opening, which will be either a story, a statistic, a question, or simply your Premise, explicitly stated.

What's next: You've grabbed your audience's attention and secured their commitment to engage by demonstrating relevance, but this isn't enough. The audience's next question is, *Does this really matter?* Chapter 10 shows you how to establish Stakes—making it clear what happens if they don't heed what you're saying.

10

Remind Them Why They (Should) Care

Our fridge's water dispenser has never worked. It was broken when we bought the house, but the fridge was otherwise in good shape. It kept cold stuff cold, yada yada. I called in a fridge-repair guy who evaluated the situation, told us the water line was broken and how much it would be to fix it. Definitely more than we wanted to spend fixing an old fridge. And besides, the water line isn't a critical function, right? So we figured we'd just fix it down the road, or eventually replace the fridge altogether.

Then one day I got home from a cross-country trip to discover water all over the kitchen floor, dripping through the woodwork into the basement. This time we paid to fix the fridge. Plus an additional fee for immediate service. Plus a week of cleaning up water and drying out the basement. And so six years later, when we moved into a new house and discovered that *that* fridge's water line was also broken, I bought a new fridge on day one.

Establish the Stakes

Your opening conveys relevance: why the audience should look up from their phones and pay attention. But just because the topic is relevant to them, doesn't mean they want to do anything about it. The next question every listener naturally asks themselves is, *Does it really matter? It's annoying, but is it worth fixing? Maybe it's worth fixing, but is it worth fixing now?* What they're asking here is what's at stake.

When I first encountered a broken water dispenser, I didn't feel the need to address the problem, because I didn't appreciate what was at stake. People don't take action unless they are motivated to, so you need to establish the Stakes immediately after the Premise.

I am not suggesting that you "raise the stakes." That's a phrase we often hear among dubious salesmen and internet marketing gurus, and they usually mean something like, "Describe in excruciating and emotionally gripping detail the worst possible outcome of not buying our thing." It's cheap, it's mean, and, more importantly, it's unnecessary. If you've already established a premise that the audience cares about, they do not need you to exaggerate what's at stake, let alone dig a knife into their side. Most often, the audience simply needs to be *reminded* of what's at stake. In other cases, you need to state it as a matter of fact.

During our first water dispenser incident, it would have been helpful for someone to say, "You know, given the condition of this hose, you're likely to have a leak that could damage your floors." I thought the worst problem I had was that we didn't have a working dispenser; it never occurred to me how bad things could get, and how quickly. But the second time? I didn't need anyone to raise the stakes. I knew what they were and that motivated me to act fast.

Stakes stem from fears

If this conversation about stakes is starting to feel familiar, it should. Back in Chapter 6 we identified your audience's primary fear. People mostly want to avoid their fears—and whatever they're trying to avoid happening, that's what's at stake.

So what's likely to go wrong, soon, if your audience doesn't get what they want, or overcome their problem? What are they afraid is going to happen, or not happen? Stakes can be phrased like this:

- "If we don't get X, then Y won't happen."
- "If we don't solve X, then Y is likely to happen."

Jot a few ideas down, but be gentle. The biggest mistake speakers and indeed all communicators make when laying out the stakes is making the situation sound dire, either by exaggerating (which is lying) or playing out a ripple effect too far down the time horizon.

Take, for example, a climate communicator who, just minutes into a keynote, tells us that if we don't stop using plastic straws immediately then the Earth will heat up, New York will be submerged in water, all the dolphins will die, and the air will become unbreathable for our great grandkids. That speaker is going to lose the audience.

Even if it were true, it's too much. Humans are wired to focus on the here and now. We just need to get them to focus on something substantial, but not overwhelming—something that's realistically likely to go wrong, soon.

So how do you establish the Stakes? Like with the Premise, there are many tactics you can use to establish the stakes. But in our work, we see facts, stats, and studies work really well. Let's look at each in turn.

Facts

In Erika's talk on success for high achievers, she lays out the Stakes in a single sentence:

> "Recent studies show that almost half of US workers feel burned out or close to it."

She could have provided the source, or the precise numbers. But unless you're dealing with a highly technical audience, they really don't care. You don't need to prove anything here, simply remind people why it matters that they pay attention.

In Dr. Blueweiss' talk on balance, she takes a matter-of-fact approach:

> "Falls are the leading cause of injury and injury-related death in the sixty-five and older population."

In Peder's talk on forgiveness, he lays out the Stakes in a similar fashion:

> "We all know, deep down, that taking responsibility for our actions is the key to long-lasting relationships."

The implication in that sentence is clear: don't want your relationships to fall apart? You have to learn how to take responsibility for your actions when you screw up.

Facts make for good Stakes, and their dryness is actually useful for not overwhelming the audience with engagement-killing emotion.

Stats and studies

Mike Shoreman is a disabled adventurer and mental health advocate, the first person with physical disabilities to paddleboard across all five Great Lakes—the largest group of freshwater lakes on Earth, situated on the border of the United States and Canada. In his talk on mental health and resilience, he combined statistics with personal reflection to soften the heaviness of the data:

> "Up to twelve people die in Canada by suicide every single day. It's the leading cause of death for those aged ten to fourteen. I was lucky; I was able to get professional help. But many people can't. Mental health challenges are so widespread that there simply isn't enough official support to help people through them. So even if they looked for the help—which many people don't—they might not get it time."[13]

Meanwhile, in my keynote on human connection, I use stats to make a light-sounding topic of human connection feel more real and present:

> "A recent study showed that more than one out of every two Americans feel lonely or isolated on a regular basis. That means even if you feel that way, at least one other person at your table does as well. And if you don't, there's a good chance at least one person sitting right next to you does."

It's the only time in the entire sixty-minute talk that I mention the loneliness epidemic. As a former entertainer, I'm booked as a kickoff keynote speaker to set the tone for the event, so I can't go dark or overly negative. And yet I learned early in my keynote career that without stakes, the talk lacks urgency. Sure, human connection is nice. But does it really need my attention at this moment? Yes, yes it does, and I'll tell you why.

Societal or non-human stakes

Not all topics are about individuals; some are about societies or communities. And not all topics are about humans; some are about animals, nature, or space. For talks in this category, it can seem impossible to identify stakes that will matter to the people in the audience who are not experts already immersed in the content area.

This is a famously tricky challenge for climate communicators. The real-world impact of our failure to take action can be decades or centuries out—there's no sense of urgency. But that's not really true. It only *feels like* there's no urgency because most climate communicators have established the wrong premise. The average person doesn't sit around worrying about the future of the planet. They've got too many immediate concerns in their life. So, how do you solve a problem like Mari… er, climate change stakes?

That's what Peder and I had to figure out. Remember Peder, who gave the TEDx talk on forgiveness? He spent over a decade as a PR expert who primarily worked on climate change communication. We discovered studies on the effect of peer influence when purchasing an electric vehicle. According to one study, people are more likely to consider and ultimately adopt electric vehicles if their neighbors already have one.[14] Ding ding ding!

What's at stake for people if they don't buy an electric car? Not just the future of Planet Earth, but their own status in the community. Any marketing or salesperson will tell you that status is a significant driver (pun intended) of purchasing decisions. A keynote speech is a sales pitch for an idea. They're not buying from you, but you do want them to buy in. And if nothing's at stake, or if the stakes don't feel present, they have no reason to care.

Example: How Dr. Levenson made animal tracking matter

Dr. Jacob Levenson's talk was about better animal tracking technology to protect ocean wildlife that eventually reaches our food supply, economy, and clean air. The key word here is "eventually."

If you recall, we made his talk relevant by framing it around protecting things we care about, and the problem of trying to protect things that don't stand still. But what about the stakes? It's subtle, and we snuck it in:

> "The ocean is made up of systems that change not over millions of years, or even hundreds of years, but often within hours, sometimes within minutes."

Can you think of anything else that moves that quickly, that you might want to protect? (I ask as my five-year-old yells "Sonic speed!" and dives off the couch, missing cracking his head on the tile floor by millimeters.) Yes, I can think of things that move quickly that I'd like to protect—and so can the audience.

YOUR TASK

Identify what's at risk if your audience doesn't tackle the problem your talk addresses.

Use the prompts:

- What's the cost of inaction? (In terms of money, time, health, relationships, or opportunity.)
- What does the fear you identified in Chapter 6 look like in reality?
- What facts, statistics, or consequences make the problem urgent?
- If someone ignored this problem for five months, or five years, what would happen?

Write one to three sentences that make the stakes explicit and personal to your audience.

Visit https://clarityupconsulting.com/opk to access a companion resource hub with worksheets, prompts, and links to supporting resources like podcast episodes and articles.

Summary

Where you are: You've established the stakes. Your audience now understands that this topic is not just relevant (premise), but that it's urgent (stakes). They know what's at risk if they don't address this problem.

What's in your outline: Under "Stakes" in your OPK outline, you now have a few sentences that make clear what happens if the audience doesn't address the problem you've identified, quoting key facts, statistics, or consequences that connect to their core fear.

What's next: Your audience knows this matters and it's urgent. Very soon they'll be asking, "But why should I listen to *you* about this?" And your answer will be a story. But we need a bridge from the stakes to your story. Chapter 11 teaches you a narrative tool that helps you to frame your entire talk with a Core Question—and position yourself as the guide who will answer it.

11
Frame Your Talk With A Core Question

Dr. Levenson has a problem. We've (finally) figured out his premise and laid the stakes—we all want to protect things we care about, but the ocean changes too quickly to use traditional methods of protection, which directly affects our food, air supply, and economy. But he's about to launch into twelve minutes of animal telemetry history and science. No matter how well we've laid the foundation of the talk, or how much we simplify the complex language around animal tracking technology, there will always be a danger of losing the audience in foreign territory.

Dr. Jake needs to give his listeners a way to stay oriented at all times. He's got a filter statement, serving as his personal compass, his North Star guiding him as he builds and delivers his speech. But what can we give the audience to serve as theirs?

My colleague Tamsen Webster, founder of the Message Design Institute and one of my fellow co-founders in the core messaging discipline, calls this kind of question a "core question." According to Tamsen, "If you're trying to figure out the best place to start or anchor your message of change, the answer is always, 'Start with the question you *exist* to answer.'"[15]

In essence, it's a version of the question they might search for that led to our known want from Chapter 4. Put differently, you need to be able to imagine your ideal audience asking this question to a trusted colleague, and that colleague saying, "Oh, at X conference last year I heard an amazing talk about this."

As we discovered in Chapter 8, rhetorical, leading, and superficial questions typically fail to engage an audience. They're either manipulative, dismissive, or just plain distracting. But the Core Question in your OPK is different, because it reveals an information gap. It's a question that is, by definition, designed for the audience to try to answer. So they will try to answer it in their own heads, only to realize they're not really sure—which means they need a guide to help them work through it. But not just any guide; they need *you*.

The Core Question is the single question your entire talk serves to answer. It creates an open loop in the audience's mind—a question they can't help but want answered—and everything that follows becomes the answer. Without it, your audience might understand each individual point you make but lose sight of where you're taking them. With it, they know exactly what journey they're on and can follow you all the way to the end.

Qualities of a Core Question

A good Core Question does two things:

- **Creates internal dialogue:** It invites the audience to start trying to answer the question for themselves, creating a sense of collaboration between you and them.
- **Leads naturally to your Story Hook:** It sets you up to share the story of how you became the person qualified to deliver the talk you're currently giving. (We'll tackle this in the next chapter.)

To craft an effective Core Question, start by rooting it in the want, problem, and stakes you've already outlined. For example, instead of asking, "Why haven't you fixed this yet?"—which could feel accusatory—you might ask, "So, how do we rebuild trust with a team when it feels like it's been broken beyond repair?"

A Core Question also needs to feel elusive but answerable. The best questions are actionable, like, "How do we make meaningful connections in a world that feels increasingly isolated?" These questions don't just make the audience curious; they align with their immediate concerns and goals.

Finally, simplicity is key. A well-crafted Core Question is short, clear, and conversational. Avoid overly complex phrasing or technical jargon, which might alienate your audience. The best questions feel like something the audience might have wondered themselves, even if they haven't consciously articulated it yet.

When you pose a question that meets these criteria, you create an immediate sense of anticipation.

Example: Dr. Levenson provides a compass

At this point in his talk, Dr. Levenson has just established that some things are hard to protect because they move and change, like the ocean's features and creatures—e.g., whales travel thousands of miles across international boundaries, and oil spills spread with shifting currents. Before diving into the history and science of animal tracking technology, he takes just eight seconds to ask the Core Question:

> "But how do you protect something that
> changes that quickly, and that unpredictably?"

Everything that follows—the history, the technology, the solution—answers this question. For the rest of the speech the audience can always return to this question in their mind as a guiding light. Anytime they drift away, they can remind themselves that we're discovering how to protect something that changes quickly and unpredictably.

More examples of Core Questions

Erika Coleman, in her talk on success for high achievers, asked, "Is there a way to accomplish all the things we need to, without paying such a high price?"

What a great question. I'm instantly trying to figure out how to do that, rattling through all the ways I've tried, and failed, to achieve my goals at a level I'm proud of without destroying myself in the process.

Our balance expert, Dr. Blueweiss, asked:

> "Many of us assume that as we get older, we inevitably get more frail. But what if aging and frailty are not synonymous?"

The audience is forced to think about ways that they might avoid getting frail as they get older, perhaps for the first time.

Another client, Dr. Yasmine Saad, is a renowned psychologist who blends eastern philosophy with western practice. Her entire introduction, up and through the Core Question, took just four lines:

> "What's wrong with me?"
> "Will they criticize me?"
> "I am not good enough."
> "Why do we get negative thoughts like these?"

She handled the premise and the stakes by simply stating some of our most pervasive, destructive internal thoughts out loud. And then she asked, "Why do we get negative thoughts like these?" That's it, the question her talk serves as the answer to.

I recommend you watch Dr. Saad's talk at TEDxOltrarno, "How to make sense of your negative thoughts."[16] It was chosen for an Editor's Pick and, at the time of writing this, has nearly half a million views just six months after being published.

YOUR TASK

It's time to craft your Core Question.

Take a moment to reflect:

- What is the known want you've identified for your audience?
- What is the problem or obstacle stopping them from getting what they want?
- What's at stake if they don't overcome this obstacle?

Now, with those answers in mind, think of questions that would address those desires and concerns. Then test them against this Core Question checklist and decide on the best one:

- Does it spark internal dialogue?
- Does it have an answer that isn't immediately obvious?
- Is it short, clear, and conversational?

When you have it, write it in the "Core Question" section of your OPK outline.

Visit https://clarityupconsulting.com/opk to access a companion resource hub with worksheets, prompts, and links to supporting resources like podcast episodes and articles.

Summary

Where you are: You've crafted your Core Question—the single question your entire talk serves to answer. This question does triple duty: it creates curiosity, provides intellectual structure, and positions you as a guide.

What's in your outline: Under Core Question in your OPK outline, you have the exact question you'll answer for your audience, a question that:

- Relates directly to your Premise and Stakes
- Can be answered with your Paradigm Shift and Action Step
- Invites the audience to lean in rather than tune out

What's next: You've framed the journey with a Core Question. Now your audience is asking: "Why should I listen to *you* about this?" Chapter 12 shows you how to choose a story that qualifies you to deliver this talk—and how to tell it in under two minutes.

12
Earn Trust Quickly With The Right Story

My dishwasher isn't draining. That sounds like a chapter title in a book about homeownership, but at this moment, it's my reality. Water is pooled up at the bottom of the dishwasher and I've got a kitchen full of dishes with family coming over tomorrow. I don't have time to call an appliance repair person so I'm stuck with my own tools and incredibly limited skills. In the world before the Internet I could not have owned a home.

But here I am on YouTube scrolling hundreds of results for "what to do when dishwasher isn't draining." Each of these videos is relevant. The stakes are clear. And they all directly answer the question I'm asking. Each video has slightly different approaches, suggestions, and techniques. I don't know *anything* about dishwashers, so I can't make a decision based on the suggested solution. I'm too dumb (about dishwashers). The only thing I can do is evaluate the person giving the advice: "Who are you, and why should I listen to *you*, specifically?"

I can't evaluate their technical solutions, so I evaluate their story. The guy who boasts, "I'm a licensed plumber with twenty years' experience"? Meh. But the dad who says, "Last Tuesday my dishwasher did [the exact same thing] and here's what I discovered"—that's the video I'm clicking, because he was in the same situation I'm in now and he solved the problem. He *gets* me.

The same goes for your audience. They can't always evaluate your solution—that's why they're listening to you in the first place. But they can evaluate whether you seem like someone who gets their problem and knows how to solve it. This is not to say that credentials don't matter. They do, but not yet. Credentials are impressive, but not particularly unique. There's always someone with more or better credentials than you. But there is no one else who perfectly shares your perspective—and your perspective was shaped by your story.

Your Story Hook

I'd rather listen to someone who went through this last week *and* is a licensed plumber, but given the choice, I'm much more likely to listen to someone who says, "This just happened to me and I fixed it." So before you tell me your formal credentials—degrees, licenses, certifications, fancy letters after your name—you need to make me feel like I'm in the right hands. That's what your Story Hook does. It's a story that qualifies *you* to deliver *this* talk.

You've already answered, "Should I pay attention?" and "Does this really matter?" Your audience are now fully engaged in the *topic*. But they're not necessarily committed to *you* yet. And so the next question your audience will naturally ask themselves is, *Why should I listen to you (and not someone else who is more obviously an expert or more famous than you)?*

Your task now is to earn their trust, and we'll do that on a human level—by connecting with them via a story.

Do you get it, and can you solve it?

You really don't need to be the world's best storyteller to nail the Story Hook in your keynote speech. When it comes to hooking the audience, choosing the *right* story is much more important than how you tell it.

This story must satisfy two conditions; it must convince the audience that:

1. You understand the Core Problem your audience faces
2. You are qualified to help them solve it

Donald Miller of Storybrand fame calls these criteria "empathy" and "authority." My colleague and story specialist, Francisco Mahfuz, calls them "pain" and "power." Call them peanut butter and jelly if you want, the point is, the audience needs to know both that you understand what they're going through—either because you have experienced it yourself or have deeply researched it—and that you are qualified to show them the path forward.

So, let's find that story and learn how to tell it.

How to find your Story Hook

Your Story Hook search is about identifying how you became the person who is qualified to give this talk, solve this problem, or guide the audience on this journey.

This particular story must be a personal one. Which isn't to say it has to be private, just that it should be something that happened to you, or that you witnessed or took part in. This is not the time for recalling historical events, stories of famous companies or business leaders, or rehashing someone else's research. We'll learn how to use stories like that to support the main points in our argument later. Those stories show that you are well read and make you a great dinner guest—but they do not prove that you're trustworthy.

We need the audience to trust you, so let's find the story that will build trust.

What happened that made you care about this?

Anytime we're working with a client to develop a speech on a tight turnaround, this is the question that usually gets us to the Story Hook the quickest. It's a good place to start your Story Hook search.

What happened to you, or in your life, that made you care about your topic?

We're looking for an experience, a conversation, an unfortunate incident, an accident—with characters saying and doing things. If you couldn't point a camera at it and film it for a movie scene, it's not going to work here.

My colleague Francisco Mahfuz introduced me to an exercise I now use with clients. He calls it, "First, Last, Worst, Best." It goes something like this:

At the top of a document or piece of paper write down the topic of your talk, and then each of these words down the left side of the page: first, last, worst, best. Leave space for notes under each.

Now consider your topic and ask, *When was the first time I remember encountering this topic? The last (final or most recent)? The worst? The best?*

Don't try to write an entire story or tell it perfectly, just jot down a bullet-point summary. Enough information that if I asked you to tell it to me out loud, you could do it. For example, my topic is human connection. So I would ask, "What is my first or earliest memory of human connection?" I might jot down a note about being bullied in middle school. In one particular instance, a bully waited for me after gym class and wrestled me to the ground while no one helped. I experienced an intense feeling of loneliness, a complete lack of connection. And then I'd do the same for the last, worst, and best memories.

Most speakers discover the seed of their Story Hook in "first" or "worst," as we tend to become experts in something as a result of an early life experience that set us on the path of discovery, or a bad experience that led us to right a wrong.

The three-act structure

Once you've discovered the seed of your story, you still need to figure out how to tell it.

Many speakers overcomplicate their stories, getting wrapped up in details that aren't necessary and, in many cases, overwhelm or distract the audience. But we use a simple three-act structure that always works, which I call the CCR method: context, change, result.

The CCR method

Technically, these are the only three components that you have to include in order for a story to actually be a story. "I was hungry, so I ate an apple, and now I feel better." It's not a great story, but it is, technically, a story. Plus it only took thirteen words and two seconds to tell.

Stories need not be long or even detailed to serve their purpose. You are not writing *The Lord of the Rings*; you're delivering a keynote speech designed to move people to action. Applying the CCR method to your keynote Story Hook looks like this:

- **Context:** What was going on in your life before things changed?
- **Change:** What changed?
- **Result:** What is different now that things have changed?

Three-act structure examples

The entire story can be one sentence, it can be three sentences, or it can be twelve sentences. Right now the length is not important, just that it gets across these three elements. Below are some examples of the CCR method put into action by some of our clients.

Margaret's deeply personal discovery

Dr. Margaret Rutherford is a renowned psychologist, host of the top podcast *SelfWork*, and author of *Perfectly Hidden Depression*,[17] which has been translated into over twelve languages. She's about as expert as expert gets.

But when I met her, she was just two months out from stepping onto the stage at TEDxBocaRaton, and she didn't have a script.[18] And although she is well established in her field, most audiences have never heard of Margaret, just as they've never heard of me, or perhaps you. So we needed a story that would qualify her as someone the audience *must* listen to on this topic.

"Margaret, what happened that made you care about 'perfectly hidden depression,' as you call it?" I asked her.

Here's the story Margaret told me—paraphrased and condensed, of course—broken down into the three-act structure:

- **Context:** "A woman, let's call her Natalie, talked about anxiety and having a panic attack at the office. She was confused and trying to make some decisions about her career."
- **Change:** "One afternoon, Natalie's husband called me after receiving a strange message from

her. Something in my gut told me to check on her, so I drove to their house and let myself in with the code he'd given me. I found Natalie in bed after a suicide attempt."

- **Result:** "Natalie survived that night, but the experience shook me to my core. I had missed her depression because she hid it behind a mask of perfectionism. That's how I first became aware of something I would eventually call 'perfectly hidden depression.'"

This story gives us the *why* behind Margaret's *what.* We now know why we should listen to her, specifically, about this critical mental health concern.

Dr. Rutherford opened her talk with this story and, as we learned back in Chapter 8, Erika also opened with a story. Sometimes a story works perfectly as both the opening of the talk and the trust-builder for the audience. To do this, it must have all three required components: contains the Premise, conveys understanding, and establishes authority.

Both Margaret's and Erika's stories contain the Premise of their talks, and so they work well as openers. But Jake's—which you'll read below—doesn't, so his Story Hook belongs after the Introduction and before the Argument (main body).

Jake's coincidental commute

In the original version of Jake's talk, he had pulled out the kind of personal story rooted in childhood that people often reach for: being at the aquarium as a kid and getting fascinated by what happens when fish swim out of view. It's a cute story, but it didn't really tell us why Jake is uniquely qualified to lead us on the journey of protecting the things we care about. It could have been any marine scientist's origin story.

Instead, we landed on the story of how he started collaborating with NASA and first discovered the technology that would allow for innovation in animal tracking:

- **Context:** "Eight years ago, I was a marine scientist commuting three hours a day to my job outside Washington, DC."
- **Change:** "One morning in the car, I heard an NPR radio piece about small satellites, and it occurred to me that they are small, cheap, and open-source—everything our current tracking system isn't. So I fired off an email to NASA, not expecting a reply, and ended up with a formal collaboration."
- **Result:** "With NASA, my team and I discovered a new technology called 'Time of Arrival,' leading to the biggest leap forward in animal tracking technology in decades."

It's not epic, moving, or sexy. But it's unique to Jake and builds trust with the audience. Clearly this guy is worth listening to, right?

YOUR TASK

It's time to craft your Story Hook. Choose the story that best helps the audience trust you—that convinces them that you understand their desire or obstacle, and that you're qualified to guide them on a journey to overcome it.

Then lay that story out in three steps: context, change, result.

The first time you tell this story in your keynote, don't get hung up on performance. You don't need to be dramatic or funny. Just tell the story. You'll get better at performing it over time, with reps—if that's needed at all.

Add this story in the CCR format, into the "Story Hook" section of your OPK, keeping it to between three and twelve sentences. In time, you'll be able to condense the outline to "The Mom Story" or "The Natalie Story" or "The NASA Story" and know precisely how to tell it. And, with that, you've completed your Introduction. Now it's time to design the bulk of your speech.

Visit https://clarityupconsulting.com/opk to access a companion resource hub with worksheets, prompts, and links to supporting resources like podcast episodes and articles, including a worksheet on telling your story using the CCR method.

Summary

Where you are: You've chosen your Story Hook—the personal story that qualifies you to deliver this talk. You've structured it using the CCR method (context, change, result), which gives your audience everything they need to trust you: proof that you understand their problem and that you're qualified to solve it.

What's in your outline: Under Story Hook in your OPK outline, you now have the story that will get your audience to buy into *you* as an authority on your topic, written out in three beats:

1. **Context:** What was happening before things changed?
2. **Change:** What shifted or happened?
3. **Result:** What's different now?

What's next: You've completed your Introduction. Your audience knows what this talk is about (Premise), why it matters (Stakes), what question you're answering for them (Core Question), and why they should trust you (Story Hook).

Now comes the heart of your keynote: the Argument. Part Four shows you how to dismantle the Status Quo, reveal a new way of thinking, and give your audience a clear path forward.

PART FOUR
MAKE YOUR CASE

Your audience is engaged. They trust you. Now they need a reason to change.

Most speakers jump straight from the problem to their solution. But the audience isn't ready. They're still asking, "Why can't I keep doing what I've been doing?" Or, "Are there any other ways to solve this that don't require learning something new?"

Fair questions. And until you answer these, they won't budge. This is why we call this section of your talk the Argument, because that's exactly what you're doing. You're building a persuasive case for a new way of thinking.

We're going to build your case step by step:

1. **Take a tour through existing solutions and dismantle them.** Your audience already has assumptions about how to solve this problem. You need to show them why those approaches fall short—not with blame, but with empathy.
2. **Reveal a new way of thinking.** Once their old options are off the table, introduce the Paradigm Shift—your key insight that changes how they see the problem.
3. **Support your case with evidence and creativity.** Data, stories, metaphors, demonstrations—you'll learn which tools to use and when.

Buy-in requires belief. By the end of Part Four, your audience won't just understand your idea, they'll hold the belief required to take action on it. They'll buy in.

13
Tour The Existing Solutions

Let's do a magic trick. "Here, pick a card." You remove the two of diamonds. "Now place it back in the middle of the deck. Okay, check this out. Down here in my pocket I have a playing card and it's… the two of diamonds!"

Amazing, right?

Maybe. Until you think to yourself, *I bet he's just got a duplicate of that same card, and somehow made me choose the two of diamonds with sleight-of-hand.* And so you don't experience the magic, because you think you know how it was done.

Here's the kicker: that might not even be how I did it. But it doesn't matter. As long as you *think* it's how I did it, or even that that's how I *could* have done it, you won't experience any magic.

But imagine if instead, when you chose a card, I gave you a permanent marker and asked you to write your name on it. Then when I pull it out of my pocket, you might start to think, *Hey, I bet he's just got a duplicate...* and then would immediately realize that can't be the case. Magic, right?

Well, maybe not. You'll move to a different possible solution, *Okay, not a duplicate. But maybe he hid it in his hand and snuck it into his pocket when I wasn't looking.* No magic. Still not how I did it, but again—doesn't matter.

So imagine if *instead,* when you chose a card, I had you sign it with a permanent marker and then gave you the entire pack of cards, asked you to replace your card somewhere in the middle, then shuffle them and place the cards on the table. And then I pull your card out of my pocket.

I bet he's got a duplicate—no, that can't be it. But maybe he snuck it into—no, because I was holding the cards... As you rifle through possible solutions in your mind, eliminating each possibility one at a time, you start to feel that maybe, just maybe, magic occurred.

Great magicians intuitively learn that you have to remove from the audience's mind all the possible ways the trick could have been done, even the obviously wrong ones, so that when you get to the climax of the trick—the moment of magic—they have nothing left to fall back on. That's when magic sticks. This is built into the structure of great magic tricks, and it's precisely what you must do to create magic in your talk.

The Argument

Before we dive in, let's be clear about what we're building. We call this section of your speech the Argument. But what is an argument?

An argument is a collection of ideas, presented in a specific order, that makes it feel reasonable to stop doing or thinking one thing and start doing or thinking something else. It's not a fight. It's a case—a persuasive structure that moves people from where they are to where you want them to be.

The Premise is actually the first step in your Argument, because it lays the foundation. You've already done that, back in the Introduction, and so when you reach the main body of your speech, you pick up where the Premise left off, by addressing what the audience is already doing to try to get what they want, or to solve their problem.

What are the common, obvious, or existing solutions to this problem? After you've introduced the problem but before you've revealed a solution, your audience will ask themselves a dangerous question: *Why can't I keep doing what I've been doing?*

People would rather do nothing—or at least continue doing what they're already doing—than try something new. New feels risky. We need to make that risk feel worth the effort.

The first time I met Dr. Levenson, he talked for hours about how cool the new, innovative animal tracking solution was. The problem? I had no idea what made it cool, let alone better than existing solutions—because I had no reference point for what the current or traditional system was, how it worked, and where it failed. We knew his audience would have the same problem, and so we set out to create a clear, if brisk, explanation of the existing solution and its pitfalls. I'll simply let you read this part of his script, because what he developed was masterful:

> "In the 1980s, emerging technology made it possible to attach satellite tags to animals and collect data. Unfortunately, that technology had a large degree of uncertainty—it could be off by as much as 1,900 meters.
>
> "That's twenty football fields. It's the length of the Las Vegas Strip. Imagine if you landed in Vegas and the airline told you that your luggage was somewhere on the Vegas Strip. You would rightly say, 'No, you've lost my luggage.'

> "Plus, those tracking tags were so bulky that we couldn't attach them to 68% of marine vertebrates. That means huge swaths of ocean wildlife remain a mystery.
>
> "And finally, these tracking tags take at least four minutes to determine the animal's position—and in most cases, marine animals surface for far less than that.
>
> "Shockingly, that's still the system we mostly use today."

Did you catch that? He identified a single existing approach (eighties-era satellite tags), and three reasons why it either doesn't work (can't attach to two-thirds of all vertebrates) or doesn't work as well as it should (inaccurate, and take too long). Now that the audience knows what the pre-existing state of animal tracking has been, the novel approach he's going to tell them about is more compelling.

What you're doing here, in the first step of building your Argument, is exploring the Status Quo.

Exploring the Status Quo

For this section of your talk, we need to identify your topic's Status Quo—in other words, what people are already doing (or thinking of doing) in order to solve their problem, overcome their obstacle, and ultimately get what they want.

Identify your Status Quo

Start by working through these Status Quo prompts:

- When you first encountered this problem, how did you try to solve it?
- What would someone who knows nothing about your topic assume works, but doesn't?
- What is intuitive but incorrect about your topic?
- What have experts in your field historically tried that has turned out to be wrong or incomplete?
- What are the misconceptions or misguided assumptions or beliefs about your topic?

Jot down a handful of ways that people, your industry, or society tends to try to solve the problem of your Premise.

What's wrong with the existing approaches?

There are three main ways that the Status Quo (an existing or common approach) can fail:

- It doesn't work.
- It doesn't work as well as it should.
- It works, but leads to unforeseen negative consequences.

Let's take them one by one.

It doesn't work

There are solutions that seem logical to people, but just don't work at all. These are the kinds of things you might bring up in a talk to a general audience that has a passing interest in your topic but basically zero understanding. As an example, we'll return to Erika Coleman's talk on high achievers, and what they tend to do when approaching the brink of burnout.

Erika's Status Quo: When someone is overwhelmed, well-meaning friends and family often tell them to "do less." Take a break. Take a nap. Take a vacation. Delegate. Pull back a little.

Why it doesn't work: To a high achiever, "do less" sounds like "care less," which they simply will not accept. It doesn't reduce their stress; it adds guilt on top of it. So while it *sounds* like sensible advice, it doesn't actually help the people it's meant to.

It doesn't work as well as it should

These existing solutions tend to come up in audiences that have a base-level knowledge of your topic, but only understand it at the theoretical level. Again, we have an example from Erika (there are many existing solutions to burnout).

Erika's Status Quo: The second bucket of advice is "do more." Time-management strategies. Meditation. Exercise. Yoga. Drink water. Wake up earlier. Go to bed earlier. Read more. Listen to podcasts. Eat better. Pet a dog.

Why it doesn't work as well as it should: The sheer volume of "good habits" becomes overwhelming, especially for someone already on the edge of burnout. Past a certain point, even virtuous behaviors offer diminished returns and can even become harmful. So yes, these strategies work, but nowhere near as well as most people believe, and often not in the moments when stressed-out high achievers need help most.

It works, but leads to unforeseen negative consequences

These are the solutions people rely on because they've actually lived inside the problem. They've tried these approaches in real life, and in the short term they might work. But over time, they backfire.

Erika's Status Quo: If you can't do less and you can't do more, high achievers often try to "do right." They try to set the correct priorities. Focus on what matters most. Give everything they have to the people and projects they value. And it does work. For a while.

The unforeseen consequences: Erika believed she was doing exactly what a responsible leader and daughter should do: prioritizing her mom, her team, and her mission. But the pace at which she was giving eventually cost her her health, her business, and her ability to keep going. "Doing right" becomes self-sacrifice. And when high achievers give everything, they have nothing left.

YOUR TASK

Identify the Status Quo—the existing or common solutions people already use (or assume will work) to solve the problem of your premise.

Use these prompts to help you find your Status Quo:

- When you first encountered this problem, how did you try to solve it?
- What would someone who knows nothing about your topic assume works, but doesn't?
- What beliefs about your topic are intuitive but incorrect?
- What have experts in your field historically tried that turned out to be wrong or incomplete?

Jot down a handful of ways that people, your industry, or society, try but fail to solve the problem of your premise. Then pick two to four to write down in your OPK outline.

Visit https://clarityupconsulting.com/opk to access a companion resource hub with worksheets, prompts, and links to supporting resources like podcast episodes and articles, including a worksheet on identifying Status Quo solutions.

Summary

Where you are: You've identified the existing solutions your audience is already trying or considering. These are approaches that seem reasonable—the things they'd find if they searched online about the problem or asked a well-meaning friend.

What's in your outline: Under Status Quo in your OPK outline, you now have a handful of "solutions" that are already out there. Don't evaluate them yet—we'll get to that.

What's next: Naming the Status Quo isn't enough. Your audience will cling to these familiar approaches unless you show them why they fall short. In Chapter 14, you'll dismantle each one—not with blame, but with empathy—until your audience has nothing left to fall back on. Then they'll be ready to hear your solution.

14
Dismantle The Status Quo

In the previous chapter you established the common ways that people, industries, or societies tend to try to solve the problem of your premise. And you've also identified, for yourself, why they either don't work, don't work as well as they should, or work in the short term but lead to unforeseen negative consequences.

Now we need to *use* this information. To do that, we're going to empathize with the audience. The Status Quo section of your keynote is not about blame, but empathy. The goal isn't to shame or blame the audience for thinking the existing (inadequate) solutions are good ideas. On the contrary, the vibe of this section of your talk should be, "It totally makes sense why you might try this, or think this is a good idea. Unfortunately…"

Walk your audience through the good and logical thinking that leads to each of these approaches. Then reveal, gently, why they are either incorrect or incomplete. Bonus points in this section if you have a story where you tried in earnest one of these solutions yourself and failed to achieve the desired outcome. But don't worry if not. We'll learn some ways to support each point of your Argument in Chapters 17, 18, and 19. For now, let's figure out how to structure the Status Quo part of your talk.

How to DEAL with the Status Quo

The best magicians deal with every possible explanation until nothing is left but the magic. And that's exactly what we're going to do with your audience's assumptions.

Here's how; step by step, we will:

1. **D**efine what people already believe will work
2. **E**mpathize with why they trust those solutions
3. **A**bolish those solutions by exposing their flaws
4. **L**ead them to a better way forward

Step 1: Define

Your audience isn't coming in as a blank slate. They already have some method for dealing with the problem your talk addresses, which they believe will work. Maybe they're following industry best practices. Maybe they've read a bestselling book. Maybe they have their own homegrown hacks. Maybe their best friend's mom told them something forty years ago and it stuck.

That's your job: list out all the common approaches people take to this problem. You did this in the previous chapter, so let's move to Step 2.

Step 2: Empathize

Don't attack them outright. Instead, empathize with people and show them why these solutions seem like good ideas.

If you start by mocking or outright dismissing a solution the audience already believe in, they will tune out immediately. Instead, you need to make it clear that these solutions seem like genuinely good ideas, and that they are reasonable to try them or believe that they'll work. Demonstrate that you understand their approach, even if it's wrong. This is where stories are useful, particularly personal stories of you trying one of these approaches yourself.

Step 3: Abolish

Now you need to show them why, actually, these approaches aren't good ideas. For each common solution, set out:

- Why it doesn't work as well as people think
- What unintended consequences it leads to
- How it might create short-term relief but leads to long-term failure
- Why it is fundamentally flawed for this particular audience

Use the above angles to reveal how each of these ineffective (but understandable) approaches falls short. This is a great time to turn to studies, data, or, again, stories, to support your points.

Step 4: Lead

The best Status Quo sections don't merely remove options, but move the audience in the right direction. Since they already trust you (thanks to the Story Hook) and they're out of alternatives (thanks to the Status Quo), they'll be willing to follow you to a new place.

This is often accomplished by recapping the Status Quo section, i.e., "So we know that X, Y, and Z don't work…" followed by a simple transition line, such as, "So, what can we do?" or "What do we do instead?" You're inviting them to discover a better way forward.

How Dr. Heather Finley DEALs with traditional gut health advice

Dr. Heather Finley is a renowned gut health specialist and founder of gutTogether®, whose work primarily supports women with bloating and chronic constipation. She often speaks about the link between mental health and gut health. Here's an example of how to build an argument, taken from the outline of one talk we worked on together.

First, she **defines** the landscape:

> "Since mental health clinicians are not gut health specialists, they tend to take one of two different approaches. Either one, ignore the GI symptoms and blame it on the eating disorder, or two, refer the client to a GI doctor."

Dr. Finley then **empathizes** with existing approaches, demonstrating that she understands the issue at hand:

> "For twelve years I was a private practice dietitian. My clients struggled with both eating disorders and digestive issues. But I didn't know enough about gastrointestinal health to

> help these clients. So most days I felt stuck, frustrated, and inadequate."

She then **abolishes** the typical approaches:

> "Studies show that 98% of individuals with disordered eating meet the criteria for a functional gut disorder. In other words, something is physically wrong in the gut, in addition to their mental health challenges like stress and anxiety. While reducing stress and anxiety is useful, it is an incomplete solution."

And while referring patients to a GI specialist seems like a great idea, in her words:

> "Western GI docs often know nothing about eating disorders and tend to prescribe Miralax as a permanent solution."

Finally, Dr. Finley **leads** them by offering a way forward in the form of a Paradigm Shift, which is the topic of our next chapter.

Give the Status Quo its due

In any given thirty-minute keynote, I'd expect this section to take between five and eight minutes. In a sixty-minute keynote, the Status Quo section may take as long as fifteen minutes. The point is, it's not a throwaway section. It's both substantial and critical.

But of course, there's always an exception. Dr. Yasmine Saad, who we met back in Chapter 11, powered through the Status Quo section in just fifty seconds:

> "In the last seventeen years working as a psychologist, my team and I have helped over 3,300 people with negative thoughts. In that time, I have seen three ways people deal with negative thoughts. One: accept them, take them at face value, and drown in the negative. Two: ignore them, let them pass like clouds in the sky. Or three: replace them with positive thoughts. Whether you accept them, ignore them, or replace them, your perspective remains that your negative thoughts are detrimental to you and you have created an enemy within."

Quite an economy of words.

YOUR TASK

Establish the Status Quo. What are the existing or common ways people try to solve the problem of your talk? Write them down.

Then, for each one—think: why doesn't it work, work as well as it should, or work but lead to unintended negative consequences? Write this down too.

Take your time here, it really matters that you get this right and do a thorough job of dismantling the Status Quo, or your audience won't be willing to take your advice or consider your new approach. In your outline under "Status Quo," write two to four current solutions and why they don't work or aren't good enough.

Visit https://clarityupconsulting.com/opk to access a companion resource hub with worksheets, prompts, and links to supporting resources like podcast episodes and articles, including an article I authored on the DEAL framework.

Summary

Where you are: You've completed your Introduction—your audience knows what this talk is about, why it matters, what question you're answering, and why they should trust you. Now you've dismantled the Status Quo, showing them why the obvious solutions won't work. This means they're out of alternatives and will be ready to hear what you have to say.

What's in your outline: Under Status Quo in your OPK outline, you now have a handful of existing but inadequate or ineffective approaches that your audience may already have tried. You should also add a line or two on why it makes sense that they'd try these (empathy). You can expect this section to take up five to eight minutes in a thirty-minute keynote—it's substantial and critical.

What's next: Your audience is in a vulnerable position—they know the problem is urgent, but every approach they can think of has been eliminated. Now they're asking: "What's the solution then?" Chapter 15 shows you how to answer that question not with a tactic, but with a Paradigm Shift—a new way of thinking that makes your solution inevitable.

15
Reveal A New Way

In 2019, I attended Seth Godin's "The Freelancer's Workshop." During one of his presentations, Seth said something like this:

> "So many freelancers complain about their clients. They complain that they're hard to work with, constantly haggle, or can't afford their fees. But that's stupid. You're self-employed; you get to choose your clients."

The words "You get to choose your clients" hit me like a lightning bolt. It was an "aha" moment that completely changed my career. Before that moment, I'd assumed that clients dictated my career. That I had to take whatever work I could get, even if it paid poorly, drained my energy, or made me miserable. But Seth shattered that belief and replaced it with a stronger, more empowering one: "Your clients don't choose you. You choose your clients."

It shifted my perspective from scarcity to control. Within months, I had completely transformed my business.

Don't jump straight to a solution

For the first time in this entire process, we will not be answering the audience's question. At least, not exactly.

If you've sufficiently dug them into a hole with your Status Quo section they'll naturally ask, "What's the solution then?" This is the wrong question. They just don't know it.

As an expert, you can probably tell people about your solution in great detail. Most of us are pretty good at explaining our solution, because it's the thing we've spent the most time thinking about. But something weird happens when you tell people how to solve their problem: they feel like they're being sold to, influenced, or forced to do something. And that makes them skeptical.

Your solution may be a tactic, a new piece of technology, a question to ask themselves or others, a proprietary framework in the form of an acronym, a new routine, or even a physical product. If I attended a presentation on lead generation, for example, most marketing gurus would immediately give me solutions—"Here's a new piece of software for scraping leads from LinkedIn," or "Use this five-step system for finding better clients."

But Seth didn't offer me a solution. There were no tools, tactics, or acronyms. Instead, he *changed the way I think* about client acquisition. And once I made that mental shift, I was finally open to exploring the various solutions to my problem, and ready to implement them.

What your audience wants is a solution. What they need first is a Paradigm Shift.

How to structure a Paradigm Shift

Every Paradigm Shift is some version of, "It's not X, it's Y."

And yes, if you're reading this in a world where AI tools like ChatGPT still exist, you're probably a bit allergic to the "It's not X, it's Y" structure, because LLMs (large language models) overuse them. The fix for that is simple: Use paradigm shifts sparingly—once per talk (or once per big idea). And only use this rhetorical device when you're offering a true shift in thinking.

But you may not immediately have a paradigm shift in mind. Instead, you probably have a solution to the problem your talk sets out to answer. As a human connection speaker, I have many solutions to the problem of feeling disconnected, lonely, or isolated. I've got conversation starters, curiosity-based questions you can ask mid-conversation to move from small talk to big talk, and even a four-step framework for mastering the art of active listening that spells out EARS (clever, right?).

But these are solutions. Tactics. Before the audience will accept any of these suggestions or be willing to risk putting them into practice, I need to get them thinking differently about human connection.

How to extract a Paradigm Shift from your solution

If you already have a solution, framework, or method, use this step-by-step process to reverse engineer the Paradigm Shift behind it.

Step 1: State your solution as simply as possible

If you had ten seconds to tell someone how to solve this problem, what would you say? Strip away all the fluff, you just want the core idea.

Erika, our expert on stress and success for high achievers, would say something like: "Get everything done that needs to be done, without sacrificing your ability to do your best again tomorrow."

Step 2: Revisit the core belief your audience holds

Back in Chapter 6 we identified your audience's beliefs. Which of these deeply held pre-existing assumptions is fundamentally holding them back from taking action?

For example, Erika's audience believes that to be successful, they must give their all.

Step 3: Frame the shift using one of these structures

Now that you know what assumption you're challenging, flip it on its head using one of these formulas:

- [Topic] isn't about X. It's about Y.
- The problem isn't X, it's Y.
- You can do X without Y.
- Stop X and start Y.

And so Erika's magnificent paradigm shift became: "You don't have to give your all to give your best."

As a card-carrying overachiever myself, it lands hard.

Here are some more Paradigm Shift examples from our clients:

- Dr. Yasmine Saad: "Negative thoughts are not enemies; they are messengers delivering information."
- Mike Shoreman: "It's not about the one in five people struggling with mental illness, but the other four people who can provide support."
- Peder Tellefsdal: "It's not about doing the right thing in the big moments, but the small moments."
- Carey Thiel and Christine Dorchak: "Successful activism is not about changing minds, but changing the law."
- Nash Fung: "We are most helpful to those in crisis not by offering solutions, but offering support."[19]
- Dr. Jacob Levenson: "Rather than tags listening for signals coming down from satellites, we can transmit signals from the tags up to the satellites."
- Brian Miller (that's me!): "We need to stop having transactions and start having interactions."

From thinking differently to doing differently

Once you've delivered your Paradigm Shift, you've earned the right to share your solution.

Yes, finally! You have my permission to talk about your framework, your methodology, your novel approach, your proprietary system—the thing you've been wanting to tell them about since you started building this talk. They're ready to hear it now because you've changed how they think about the problem.

Without the shift, your solution would have felt like just another option. With it, your solution feels inevitable, so it's the perfect time to tell them about that four-step framework, your novel medicine, or your company's proprietary algorithm. In Chapter 16 you'll discover two different structures for explaining your solution within the context of the Argument you've been building.

What an Argument looks like

"Hi, sir, new to the neighborhood?"

I look up from buckling my four-year-old into his car seat as a teenager who could only have graduated high school last week walks up my driveway. He's wearing tan khaki pants and a black polo shirt with a company logo on it. I thought door-to-door salesmen were extinct.

"Yeah," I reply briskly. "We just moved in a few weeks ago."

"Welcome to the area!" he smiled. "The mosquitos are terrible though."

Look at that. A Premise in the wild.

I nod, "Yup. They're something else. Much worse than up north. My kid is getting eaten alive."

"And your house backs up to the creek, right? They must be terrible out back. Can't be much fun sitting on your deck or playing in the backyard. How are you planning to deal with that?"

Want. Problem. Stakes. Question.

OK, mosquito man. You've got me.

"Well, back in Connecticut we had regular spraying from a company like yours. Go ahead, tell me about what you do."

"Some folks don't do anything, but if you back up to the creek, you're going to have a very hard time. We do your next-door neighbors—have you met the Hendersons yet? Super nice folks, we've been doing their lawn for years. Anyway, that's how I know how bad it is back there."

A mini Story Hook—he's establishing understanding and authority. This pitch is so beautiful I might cry. He continues with the Status Quo:

"And then some folks only spray the perimeter of the yard. Which is fine if you're only worried about mosquitos, but in this area you've got all kinds of other annoying critters."

He lists a bunch of weird southern bugs that I'd already seen, and conveniently hid from my wife who, if she'd encountered them, would have immediately sold the house we'd just purchased.

"So we spray the lawn too," he continues, "all the way up to the house and around the perimeter."

I nod again. "Sounds pretty intense."

"Actually, our approach is pretty cool. We do an environmental scan of your house and create a solution specific to the exact bugs and critters you're dealing with. So instead of guessing and spraying for everything, our service is targeted and custom."

And there it is, a Paradigm Shift. But my kid is getting antsy and we need to get moving.

"Okay, this sounds great. What's the deal if I want to do it?"

He hit me with a simple Action Step, and a picture of Success—which we'll cover in Part Five.

"Super easy. Here's a brochure. Just scan the QR code or give us a call and we'll schedule the evaluation date to get started. Then you can enjoy your beautiful new yard with your family."

That's what it looks like to make your case. This almost-a-young-adult successfully took me from a stranger who wasn't even thinking about hiring a lawn spraying service to being ready to swipe my credit card in under three minutes while buckling my kid into the car.[20]

YOUR TASK

Take a good look at your solution to the audience's Core Problem. It may be a tactic, a new piece of technology, a question to ask themselves or others, a proprietary framework in the form of an acronym, a new routine, or even a physical product.

Pull out the Core Belief preventing them from moving forward, and identify the new, stronger belief that would have to replace it in order for them to be open to your solution.

Phrase it using one of these variables:

- "[Topic] isn't about X; it's about Y"
- "The problem isn't X; it's Y"
- "[Core Belief] isn't inevitable; it's [new belief]"

Make it punchy, memorable, and quotable. This is the line people will remember and repeat. Now write it in your outline in the "Paradigm Shift" section, along with a few bullet points about the solution you're going to deliver—don't worry too much about how it fits in the outline. You're about to learn two different ways to structure it, and how to identify which is right for your talk.

Visit https://clarityupconsulting.com/opk to access a companion resource hub with worksheets, prompts, and links to supporting resources like podcast episodes and articles, including a worksheet on extracting a Paradigm Shift from your solution.

Summary

Where you are: You've identified your Paradigm Shift—the single reframe that changes how your audience thinks about the problem. This isn't a tactic or tool; it's a fundamental shift in perspective that makes your solution feel obvious rather than forced.

What's in your outline: You have now addressed your audience's pre-existing beliefs and reframed the problem they're facing with a Paradigm Shift using a clear structure that leaves no room for doubt. This sets your Argument up for success.

What's next: You've introduced a Paradigm Shift, but how does your solution fit into the mix? Now, finally, your audience will be ready to receive the tactical solution you want to offer them. Chapter 16 will help you choose between the macro structure (one solution for everything) and the micro structure (individual solutions for each problem), which will determine how the rest of your Argument unfolds.

16

Choose A Structure For Your Argument

Once you've shaped your solution into a Paradigm Shift, you may wonder, *But hang on—what if I have more than one solution in my talk? Do I need a new Paradigm Shift for each one?*

The answer is probably not. Most talks delivered by experts should center on one Paradigm Shift—that's the core of your Argument.[†]

† More accurately, you want one Paradigm Shift per big idea. I suggest that you spend twenty to thirty minutes per big idea, which means for most folks reading this book, you'll only be delivering one big idea in your talk, and therefore only need one Paradigm Shift. But if you're delivering a forty-to-sixty-minute keynote, you may have two or at most three big ideas. In that case, you'll want to complete a full Argument (Premise, Status Quo, Paradigm Shift, Action Step, Success) for each big idea. In those situations, the conclusion of your first big idea typically becomes the Premise of your next big idea. This is an advanced speech design technique, which is why I have relegated it to a single footnote rather than an additional chapter on how to structure such talks.

The real question is how to present your solution, or solutions. Do you have one solution that resolves all the problems your audience is facing? Or do you need to walk them through separate solutions for each problem? The answer determines your structure:

- **Macro structure:** One Paradigm Shift, one solution that addresses multiple problems
- **Micro structure:** One Paradigm Shift, with individual solutions for each problem

In most cases, this choice will reveal itself to you, because it's less of a decision and more of an examination. If you've got one big solution, it's macro. If you have multiple smaller or individual solutions, it's micro.

Let's do a deep dive into each structure first, then we'll talk about the ambiguous or edge cases when it's not totally clear which to use.

The macro shift structure: One solution to rule them all

This works best when your audience holds multiple flawed beliefs (the Status Quo) that all stem from a single deeper issue. Instead of challenging each belief separately, you present them together, exposing how each one fails. Once the audience sees that none of their assumptions holds up, you introduce a single

Paradigm Shift that reframes the entire problem and renders all those beliefs obsolete, and follow that up with a solution for implementing this new way of thinking.

Let's take Erika's talk as an example. A quick review of her Argument reveals a macro shift structure:

Premise: We all want to be seen as competent and capable, but in an effort to achieve success we tend to overwork, which can lead to exhaustion.

Status Quo:

- Approach one: Do less.
- Approach two: Do more.

Both approaches lead to failure—one feels like "care less," and the other overwhelms the already overwhelmed.

Paradigm Shift: You don't have to give your all to give your best.

Solution: The art of even-achieving—getting everything done that needs to be done without sacrificing the ability to continue doing your best tomorrow.

In Erika's case, her audience's problem stems from a single flawed belief about success: that being a high achiever requires giving everything you have, all the time. That belief fuels the two major, well-intentioned but ineffective approaches: doing less (which feels wrong) and doing more (which becomes unsustainable).

She offers a single Paradigm Shift that reframes the entire situation—success doesn't require overextending—and then introduces a solution for acting out that shift: even-achieving.

It's a powerful and elegant argument structure that works beautifully for TED-style talks and shorter keynotes when time is limited (ten to twenty minutes). But sometimes you need a different solution for each flawed existing methodology. That's when the micro structure becomes useful.

The micro shift structure: One solution per problem

This is the best structure when the audience believes in multiple flawed approaches that each need to be dismantled and replaced with a different solution.

That's how we approached Dr. Margaret Rutherford's talk on "How to recognize perfectly hidden depression." We discussed Margaret briefly in Chapter 12, when she told the story about her client, Natalie, whose depression was masked by her perfectionism. Margaret opened the talk with this, her Story Hook, as a way to implicitly state the Premise, but then followed it with an explicit Premise statement:

Premise: "We all have secrets, but it's not the secrets themselves that get us into trouble. It's our feelings about those secrets that darken and deepen over time."

Stakes: "Depression and suicide rates are going up around the world. Soon, every single one of us will either know someone personally or have heard a story about someone whose life looked great on the outside, and then died by suicide."

Core Question: "Is it possible to create a culture where revealing these secret feelings is not shameful, but is actually viewed as healthy self-awareness and personal strength?"

Once Margaret had got the audience's attention, established the Stakes, and qualified herself as a trustworthy guide, it was time to make her case. She identified three typical approaches to dealing with these kinds of mental health cases:

Status Quo:

- Therapists diagnose using the medical model lens (the DSM).
- There's a cultural taboo on suicidal thoughts.

- We blame or judge people who speak like that, even ourselves.

From here, Margaret notes that perfect-looking lives can camouflage depression, which she calls "perfectly hidden depression." And that leads to her talk's fundamental shift in thinking.

Paradigm Shift: "Revealing our secret pain is not shameful; it's strength."

Then Margaret adopts the micro shift structure to build an argument, offering an individual solution to each Status Quo problem. Here's a sketch of how she does this:

Status Quo 1: The Medical Model. Clinicians often miss perfectly hidden depression because the DSM symptom checklist doesn't account for it. We need to expand assessments to include questions about "psychache" or psychological pain.

Status Quo 2: Cultural Taboo. When we treat suicidal thoughts as abnormal or shameful, we create a culture in which people who are struggling bury and hide their pain. Instead, let's recognize that suicidal thoughts are actually a common human response to pain. Remember, it's not the secrets themselves, but the feelings about those secrets, that cause real harm.

Status Quo 3: Blame and Judgment. Friends and family have a reflexive negative reaction to any discussion of suicidal thoughts, which feels like shame to the receiver. Let's replace judgment with acceptance, compassion, and openness to allow people the space to have these difficult conversations.

This is a classic micro shift structure: one new way of thinking, but individual solutions to individual problems. Notice that in the case of a micro shift structure, you'll want to sketch the Status Quo section first, then provide the Paradigm Shift, then revisit each aspect of the Status Quo in depth in order to offer individual solutions through the lens of the shift in thinking:

1. Status Quo:
   - SQ1
   - SQ2
   - SQ3
2. Paradigm Shift
3. Status Quo revisited:
   - Solution to SQ1
   - Solution to SQ2
   - Solution to SQ3

This creates seamless transitions for the audience between parts of the talk without losing the power of the overall Argument structure.

Margaret delivered her talk at TEDxBocaRaton and at the time of writing this, the YouTube video just passed

2,000,000 views. What makes this even more impressive is that Margaret publicly admits to severe speech anxiety. While she is a world-class psychologist in one-to-one settings, she is not a natural-born public speaker. And yet she delivered this talk seamlessly, and her work is now making a bigger impact around the world than ever before.

Ambiguous cases

As stated, the decision between a micro or macro structure is often made for you. However, there are times when you could offer an individual solution to each problem, but one of those solutions is far more powerful, detailed, or in-depth than the others, causing an imbalance.

This creates a real dilemma, and it ultimately comes down to pacing versus depth. The macro structure feels faster because it minimizes the time between the audience encountering the failed approaches and discovering the solution. But the micro structure benefits from spending more time on each failed approach and how to resolve it, which can give the audience a deeper sense of understanding.

Neither is right; it can only be right for *this* talk and *this* audience.

For example, recall Dr. Levenson's talk on animal tracking. He identified three problems in the Status Quo. Traditional tags are:

- Inaccurate: Can be off by up to 1,900 meters.
- Large: Can't attach to 68% of marine vertebrates.
- Slow: Take at least four minutes to determine an animal's position.

Now, there are individual solutions to each of these problems, and Jake could have talked about each of them for a sustained period of time. But the individual solution to the accuracy problem—Time of Arrival technology—also resolves the other two. So we decided he didn't need to spend time talking about ways to make tags smaller, or how to improve the speed of determining location. Instead, he could focus on one solution, Time of Arrival. By choosing a macro instead of a micro shift structure, when either would have worked, we kept a brisk pace for a talk that otherwise may have felt overwhelming to a science-light audience.

Whereas in Margaret's talk we discussed earlier, it felt important to give the audience a deep sense of understanding on a heavy topic—by taking the typical approaches one by one, examining them, and revealing their flaws.

Visit the resource hub at the end of this chapter for a worksheet and decision tree on choosing a macro or micro argument structure for your talk.

YOUR TASK

Choose an Argument structure: macro or micro. Do you have one solution that overcomes all the flaws in the Status Quo approaches in the Status Quo, or multiple solutions to multiple flaws?

Your topic might make this choice obvious. If not, consider which would be more useful or generous to your audience: brisk pacing, or deep understanding?

And if you really can't decide, sketch out both structures and see how it feels to casually talk through them as if you had an audience. Sometimes it's hard to tell on the page how something will feel said out loud, and decisions around pacing and rhythm need extra attention.

Visit https://clarityupconsulting.com/opk to access a companion resource hub with worksheets, prompts, and links to supporting resources like podcast episodes and articles.

Summary

Where you are: You've chosen your Argument structure—either macro (one solution addresses all problems) or micro (individual solutions for each problem). You understand how your Status Quo, Paradigm Shift, and Solutions fit together to create a cohesive case for change.

What's in your outline: In your OPK outline, you have now organized your Argument section using either a macro or micro structure, unified by one Paradigm Shift.

What's next: You've built the skeleton of your Argument—the structure is solid. But right now, each point is just a claim. Your audience needs evidence. The following three chapters will show you how to support each point with data and creative tools that make your case not just logical, but compelling.

17

When And How To Use Data

I'm sweating from my forehead. Admittedly, it's my fault. I've typed "airline incidents America 2025" into Google and I'm now scrolling in the deep. It's been a pretty rough year for the airline industry, with a dozen or so notable stories. I've never been an anxious flyer. I've spent most of my life living in airports and jetsetting around the world. Plus, I know the stats.

According to the Bureau of Transportation Statistics, there are statistically 0 injuries per 100 million miles flown, compared to 42 injuries driving in cars and trucks.[21] I took a bigger risk driving to my local grocery store to pick up a particular type of salami I was craving than I will on this flight. But I'm more nervous about the flight. Because the story in my head about falling out of the sky in a burning tube of metal and gasoline is powerful, intense, and vivid in a way that statistics just aren't.

If we could simply state our points, explain the logic, and have the audience fully adopt our position, speaking would be easy.

Alas, not so.

For each point you make in the Argument, no matter how true or believable, you'll need to support it with evidence. And you've made quite a few points. You'll have at least two to three points in the Status Quo, one Paradigm Shift, and at least one solution if not multiple, depending on whether you chose a macro or micro structure.

Over the next two chapters, I'll sketch out a handful of ways to support each point, so that you can not only choose the best fit for each case, but create variety within your presentation. But let's begin with data.

Data is often necessary but not sufficient

"In this 2012 study conducted by Ms. Scientist and Mr. Academic, we see that 83% of people choose the first option when given only one option."

The audience nods, having graciously accepted that their previous assumption is disproven by a number, a percentage, some quotation marks, and a citation. All's well.

Whoops, sorry—I went to fantasy land for a second.

OK, here's the deal: facts are valuable. They support our points. They just don't tend to carry the heavy load of persuasion or influence that speakers think they do; partly because data is often cold and therefore easy to dismiss, but also because modern audiences have learned that facts can be misrepresented or misleading. Everyone pretty much understands how easy it is to "lie with statistics"—which is not to say you're doing that. It's only to say that audiences are skeptical of data alone.

Data is like a thin chip that can be dipped in salsa but can't support the weight of guacamole.

When to rely on data

So, if data alone won't move an audience, why use it at all? There are three situations where data is essential:

1. When your audience expects it
2. When you need to ground a claim
3. When you want your ideas to live beyond the room

Let's look at each of those in turn.

Audience expectation

If you're presenting to a room of academics, scientists, or engineers, data isn't optional. It's expected. "Audience first, always" means respecting the way your audience already engages with ideas.

I was once asked to speak on human connection to the global workforce at an international market research company. These folks eat, sleep, breathe, and daydream in data. So even on this emotional topic, I included far more hard evidence than I normally would. And it worked. Each time a number appeared on my slides, I saw heads nodding and phones coming out for screenshots. In that room, for that audience, the numbers brought credibility.

In our client Dr. Jacob Levenson's talk on animal tracking, he supported his Argument with this line:

> "Time of Arrival tracking is more accurate than anything we've seen. A global receiver network—including satellites, drones, buoys, and even wind turbines—shrinks the error margin from 1,900 meters to just 2 meters."

His data-led approach both respects his science-minded listeners while also grounding his claim.

Grounding a claim

Data can also be effectively used to provide context for assertions and stories that might otherwise feel like mere opinion, or unique situations that don't apply broadly. Here, data shifts your point from "this worked for me" to "this works," or from "I believe this strongly" to "this is true."

In my talk on human connection I could simply say, "We are treating interactions as transactions, and it's having a devastating impact on our lives." Maybe you believe me, maybe you don't. But when I pair it with, "According to Cigna's 2023 study on loneliness, over 50% of Americans self-report feeling lonely or isolated on a regular basis,"[22] I give my claim credibility. If you want to disagree with me, you also have to disagree with the research. That's much more difficult to do.

In Dr. Carole Blueweiss's talk on balance, she grounds the implied claim that "balance matters" with two public health data points:

> "Falls are the leading cause of injury and injury-related death among adults 65 and older."
>
> "Each year, at least one out of every four people aged 65 and older experiences a fall."

Two simple statistics shift her Argument from "this matters to me" to "this matters."

Idea longevity

Emotions engage, but they fade quickly. Numbers remain. They're what people cite to their boss, their team, or themselves later. Even if you can't remember everything I said, you can probably remember that over half of people feel lonely. And if you're an HR director, you could cite that to your boss on Monday to convince them to invest in new wellness initiatives for their employees.

In Mike Shoreman's mental health talk, the Status Quo is simple: Without realizing how common struggle is, people delay seeking help. He grounds this with one key piece of data:

> "The latest statistics from Canada and the US show that one in every five adults will struggle with mental health challenges during their lifetime."

This data sticks because it sets up Mike's Paradigm Shift: "If one person struggles, four can carry. Who are your four?"

Best practices for using data

If you're going to use data—and you should—here are some things to keep in mind.

- **Use it sparingly.** Unless you're in a data-focused room, a few well-chosen facts beat a pile of numbers.
- **Show contrast.** Old versus new, before versus after. Make the difference clear with numbers on both sides.
- **Make it repeatable.** Pick a simple stat people will remember and be able to quote tomorrow. Keep it simple, silly.

YOUR TASK

Review each point in your Status Quo, Paradigm Shift, and Solution. Identify any points that need grounding or would benefit from extra credibility, and locate the specific research finding or a statistic that supports it and write this in the relevant parts of your OPK outline. If it isn't your own research, also make a note of the source. After it, write what this stat *means* for your audience—give it context so they can connect.

Visit https://clarityupconsulting.com/opk to access a companion resource hub with worksheets, prompts, and links to supporting resources like podcast episodes and articles.

Summary

Where you are: You understand when and how to use data effectively: sparingly (unless your audience expects it), strategically (to ground claims and create repeatability), and always paired with something more emotional. Data provides credibility but rarely persuades on its own.

What's in your outline: At relevant points (likely scattered throughout), you should now have a few, "According to [Organization], [stat]" type lines in your outline to support your points and your overall Argument.

What's next: Data alone won't move your audience to action—emotion will. The following two chapters reveal six creative tools (stories, metaphors, hypotheticals, visuals, demonstrations, and interaction) that bring your points to life and make your Argument not just believable, but memorable.

18

Using Stories To Support Your Points

The world increasingly feels like an episode of *Whose Line Is It Anyway?*. Everything's made up and the facts don't matter! In this world, how do we convince our audiences—or rather, help them convince themselves—that our idea is worthy of adopting?

We support our hard data with a softer appeal to their emotions. We do this by engaging in creativity and using stories and story-adjacent techniques like metaphors and hypotheticals.

When to use stories to support your points

In Chapter 12 we learned how to choose a core story to support your talk overall, which we appropriately called the Story Hook, and a few ways to tell it. But here in the Argument we needn't be so measured.

My story specialist Francisco says, "A story is a real-life example that makes a point." So, whether you're establishing the Premise, exploring the Status Quo, or proposing a Paradigm Shift, you can always find a real-life example that "proves" your point. This may be in place of data, to explain data, or to augment it. Basically, when in doubt, tell a story.

Dr. Marjorie Aunos is a psychologist, researcher, and advocate for parents with disabilities. In a twist of fate, Marjorie became the subject of her own life's work when, as the single mother (by choice) of a young child, she was in a car accident that rendered her paraplegic. In her talk on what we can learn from parents with disabilities, she wanted to make this point:

> "Several studies on psychotherapy demonstrated that solution-focused questions lead to more positive emotions and an increase in self-efficacy, or the ability to do things for oneself."[23]

Compelling? Not really. Or at least, not on its own.

Marjorie is a natural and gifted storyteller, so we agreed that just before she delivers the research, she should tell a brief story about the time immediately following her accident. This is what we landed on:

> "In rehabilitation, I told them I wanted to push my baby in a stroller. We spent months trying to find a way that would attach a stroller to my wheelchair, so that I could use both my hands to roll. But by the time we solved the problem, my son had become this very big and strong toddler. And with his weight and mine, it was too difficult for me to go anywhere.
>
> "We had spent months coming up with a solution that could no longer be applied—because we had focused on the problem and its cause: me, not being able to push both the stroller and the wheelchair."

In 109 words and just 30 seconds, she helped the audience understand the real-world consequences of problem-solving approaches. And it perfectly sets her up for the Paradigm Shift she's about to make, giving emotional weight to the research she's going to cite.

Remember: a story needn't be long or involved. Context, change, and result is all you need—and it can be done quickly.

When to use a metaphor or hypothetical

Sometimes the stories you've lived or are familiar with don't perfectly match the point you're trying to make, or you don't feel comfortable including real people, or you have to worry about confidentiality, or you don't have a story that matches the situation of the audience. In such cases, we can rely on metaphors or hypothetical scenarios.

If a story is a real-life example that makes a point, a metaphor is a non-literal example that makes a point, and a hypothetical is an imaginary example that makes a point.

Example: Dr. Saad uses a metaphor

I first met Dr. Yasmine Saad while helping shape the idea for her future talk at TEDxOltrarno, "How to make sense of your negative thoughts," which was ultimately selected for an Editor's Pick.[24] I asked her to explain what the big deal was with negative thoughts. She immediately asked me to imagine sitting in my living room late at night… and within just sixty seconds helped me understand precisely why her idea matters. Nine months later she used the exact same metaphor on the Red Dot itself:

> "You're sitting in your living room, enjoying a great movie, and there's a bang at the door. It's probably a delivery person, but you didn't

> order anything so you just decide to ignore it, but the banging continues. Now you're getting annoyed, you can't go back to enjoying your movie, and the banging gets louder and louder.
>
> "That is exactly what happens to us when negative thoughts come knocking at our door. They are unwanted, interrupt our joy, and can create annoyance, angst, doubt and fear. We then think they are detrimental to us."

Negative thoughts are not literally intrusive knocks at a door at night while watching a movie, but that's how they feel. That's a metaphor.

Example: Dr. Saad uses a hypothetical

Later in Dr. Saad's talk, after explaining her Paradigm Shift (that negative thoughts are useful if you learn how to decode them), she uses a hypothetical to help the audience understand how this happens:

> "Let's apply this to a daily life experience. You come home from work; you had a very long day. And you see the dirty dishes in the sink.
>
> "And you're like, 'Ugh. I am so frustrated.'
>
> "So let's decode this thought together. Let's engage your inner compass: ask yourself, what is this thought calling your attention to?
>
> "You'll tell me, 'The dirty dishes.'

> "And I'll be like, 'Yeah, but let's go deeper. Why are the dirty dishes so frustrating to you?'
>
> "You'll be like, 'I work so hard. The last thing I want is to come home and work harder.'
>
> "Aha! Now we're onto something. The problem is not the dirty dishes. The problem is your life of hard work."

Imaginary scenarios engage us in a similar (although not identical) way to stories. Such hypotheticals can be very useful in supporting your Argument.

Sometimes speakers rely so heavily on stories, telling one after another for the entire talk, that the power of storytelling begins to diminish. Like any repeated exposure to the same thing, audiences can develop a sense for how stories are structured, when to expect a twist, and even predict their ending. Boring, right? Metaphors and hypotheticals exist in the same emotional space as stories but they *feel* different, and using them can bring a talk to life with variety.

But what about when you've got to relay something that feels *super boring,* like research results?

Making research more interesting

There's one more reason to tell a real story, and that's when you want to talk about the results of a study. Consider this statement:

> "A famous study shows that people are more likely to comply with a request when you offer a reason."

Not super compelling, is it? You might think, *Sure, that makes sense.* But the likelihood I'm going to engage you, let alone move you to action, based on that generic hand-wave to a study is low. So I might include some more authoritative info, like:

> "A researcher at Harvard discovered that people are 50% more likely to comply with a request when you offer a reason."

Better, for sure. But still lacking. Okay, let's try one more time:

> "In 1978 a researcher named Dr. Ellen Langer stood in the copy room at Harvard University. She's watching the behavior of students waiting in line to make copies before class, when one student walks up and tries to cut the line..."[25]

I'm going to stop there. You don't need the rest of the story to understand the point I'm making, which is simply how much more engaging it is to hear about a study in story form.

This is an actual example from my own presentations on communication, when I will occasionally refer to Ellen Langer's now-infamous Xerox study. Rather than simply telling the audience the result, I tell them about the journey she took to arrive at that result. I reveal the result of each round of the experiment as it unfolded, keeping the audience in suspense about where it's all going, much like Dr. Langer would have been in suspense not knowing how the study was going to shake out. And so when we get to the ultimate takeaway, there's context, emotional engagement, and importantly, time spent. Rather than a single sentence result that's unengaging, I get three to five minutes of entertaining stage time that still serves to make the point.

If you've got a statistic or scientific insight, dig into the story of the study itself. It's not hard these days to find Wikipedia entries, journal reports, or biographies detailing the process of creating a particular study. You can always ask an LLM like ChatGPT in "deep research" mode to find that information for you. And if you can't find anything publicly, reach out to the researchers themselves—academics are often thrilled to get on the phone or email to talk about the details of their work. When you dig into the story of the study, you might find something interesting behind-the-scenes, and your audience will thank you for it.

YOUR TASK

Identify which points in your Argument could be supported with a story, metaphor, or hypothetical.

Prompts:

- Do you have a real-life example (yours or someone else's) that illustrates this point?

- If not, is there a metaphor that captures how this feels or works?
- Could a hypothetical scenario ("Imagine you're...") help the audience experience the point?
- Are you citing research? Can you tell the story of the study instead of just stating the result?

For each major point in your Status Quo, Paradigm Shift, and Solution, note in your OPK outline which technique you'll use to support it. Remember, the idea is to make the point emotionally resonant, not just logically sound.

Visit https://clarityupconsulting.com/opk to access a companion resource hub with worksheets, prompts, and links to supporting resources like podcast episodes and articles, including a private video training on how to tell the story of a study.

Summary

Where you are: You understand how to support your points with stories (real examples), metaphors (non-literal comparisons), and hypotheticals (imagined scenarios). You know that research becomes more compelling when you tell the story of the study. And you know that variety matters—don't tell five stories in a row.

What's in your outline: Your OPK outline should now contain various notes throughout your Status Quo, Paradigm Shift, and Solution sections, e.g. "Story about X," or "Metaphor of Y" next to the relevant points.

What's next: Stories aren't the only way to make your points land. In Chapter 19, you'll learn how to use visuals, demonstrations, and direct audience interaction—these are higher-risk tools that, when used well, make audiences lean in like nothing else.

19
Visuals, Demonstrations, And Direct Interaction

Stories can be captivating, but they are not the only way to creatively support your points. You can also use visuals, demonstrations, and direct interactions. I will not spend too much time on these techniques, as they are well beyond the scope of this book. But I would be doing the topic and you an injustice if I didn't at least mention them as options of content and techniques that you can include in your keynote.

Visuals

Visuals can complement (but should never replace) data or stories. Humans are visual creatures. We like looking at pretty and interesting things. And while I'm sure you're interesting-looking, sometimes the audience just needs a visual break from staring at one person's face for an extended period.

In an attempt to make their speeches more visually interesting, most speakers open up PowerPoint and begin the slow descent into maddening, exhausting, rather-have-dental-work presentations. Listen to me on this: visuals should never, *ever*, replace your content.

If someone who didn't attend your talk could follow it by simply reading the slide deck, there was no point giving a live presentation. You can just send people the slides and save their time.

Comic strip artists will tell you that the visual and the caption work together. Either of them may be humorous on their own, but the real impact comes from taking them as a pair. It's the same with speakers and slides. If you're going to put a visual on the screen, it should add to the words you're saying, not replace them. Visuals can be particularly useful for representing complex data, or adding humor via memes, gifs, or video clips.

But by far my favorite visual technique is to use physical objects on stage. When Dr. Levenson took the stage at TEDxFoggyBottom, as I described earlier, he was holding a giant orange device with wires attached to it. I could literally hear people asking their neighbor, "What is that?" And then he delivered the opening line: "This is a Fitbit… for whales." Perfection.

During Peder's entire talk at TEDxArendal two large easels sat on either side of him, each covered in a sleek black cloth. He never mentioned or even glanced at them, keeping the audience in suspense, until two minutes from the end:

> "On the forgiveness road trip, the last person I visited was my dad. As I walked up to the house, I knew exactly how the conversation was going to go. My dad, my idol, was going to be disappointed in me. I needed him to forgive me, but I knew I didn't deserve it.
>
> "Instead, my dad commissioned two custom paintings for me. When he presented them to me, here's how he described them…
>
> [Peder reveals the blue painting]
>
> "'This, Peder, this is you rowing alone, facing the darkness, unable to see the light that is in front of the boat. You tried so hard to prove your worth, even though we never needed more proof. And over time we lost the Peder that we used to know.'
>
> [Peder reveals the red painting]
>
> "And then he said to me, 'This painting symbolizes when you finally stopped rowing. You found yourself. I had longed for you to return to us. And when you laid all the cards on the table, asking for forgiveness, I knew that my son was back.'"

Peder's plan had always been to show the paintings during the climax of his talk, but like most speakers, it never occurred to him that he could do it on stage with the actual paintings. Then one session my magician's instinct kicked in and I asked if he'd feel comfortable bringing the actual paintings to the live event. His expressive Norwegian eyebrows went up, and I could see that he immediately understood how much more powerful it would be.

It was. The audience never expects non-slide visuals, and it always makes them lean in. So consider, is there anything you're planning to put on a slide that you could physically bring with you to the speech? An easy way to include physical visuals is to draw a chart or graph in real-time rather than put it on a slide. And if you have terrible drawing skills, even better. It's more human.

Demonstrations

Demonstrations keep the audience on their toes. Where a visual is merely representative of a point, a demonstration makes the point for you. If you can prove your point live and in real-time, you're really in good shape.

During Dr. Blueweiss's talk on balance, she wanted to make the point that your body is already keeping you balanced all the time with an incredibly complex automatic system that most of us aren't aware of and often don't appreciate. As she delivers the line, "Say you're walking and someone pushes you from behind, so you take a step..." Carole throws herself forward as if she's been pushed, and you watch her right leg instinctively jump out in front of her. As she lands on her right foot, she points to it and says, "That's a good thing. That's another way you prevent yourself from falling."

Physically acting out what it looks like for your body to prevent a dangerous fall is much more engaging than simply describing what happens. Tiny moment, massive impact.

During my keynotes on human connection, I often talk about easy ways to introduce yourself to a stranger. I teach The Simple Technique, by which I mean to simply say: "Hi, I'm Brian." And sure, I could just tell the audience that it works to introduce yourself with your name. But instead of telling them, I jump off stage and walk up to someone in the front row, sticking out my hand and saying, "Hi, I'm Brian!" To which they always respond, "Hi, I'm [their name]."

"That's The Simple Technique," I then tell the audience. "When you give someone your name, the social contract kicks in and it's literally impossible for them to respond with anything other than theirs. And just like that, you're talking."

It's a ten-second live, real-time demonstration that proves my technique works and gives the audience confidence to try it for themselves during the next coffee break (thus taking action, creating buzz, and making me a hero for meeting professionals everywhere).

Direct interaction

My "Hi, I'm Brian" demonstration example also introduced one more tool us speakers can use to make our points, and that's direct audience interaction. This includes icebreakers, polls, diagnostic assessments, workshop elements like small group discussions or stand-and-shares, or even Q&A.

This is a technique to use cautiously and sporadically. Most untrained speakers are not prepared to do this and so should avoid it. It's best left to confident presenters who have a lot of on-stage experience dealing with unpredictable situations. You really don't know how the audience will react if you directly engage with them, and so you need to be prepared for anything.

I recently spoke at a major conference where the closing keynote speaker, who is a renowned, award-winning presenter with decades of experience in front of live audiences, engaged the audience in a Q&A mid-speech. But this particular audience was highly skeptical of the speaker's topic, and unafraid to tell him that. In question after question, the audience members expressed extreme and, in some cases, volatile opinions that the speaker had clearly not anticipated. He did his best to dance around them, but the damage was done and he lost the command of the room that he'd held up until that point. An attendee said to me later, "He looked like a deer in the headlights during the Q&A section."

Direct interaction is a high-risk, high-reward strategy. Interacting tells the audience that you're fully present and that this is really for them, not a canned presentation that you could give to any room. Use it if you're confident. Avoid it like the plague if you're not.

YOUR TASK

Consider whether any points in your Argument could be supported with visuals, demonstrations, or direct interaction.

Prompts:

- Is there anything you're planning to put on a slide that you could physically bring to the speech?
- Can you prove a point live and in real-time rather than just stating it?
- Are you confident enough to directly engage the audience, and to handle the unexpected? (If you have to think about it, the answer is no.)
- Does using one of these tools add to your words, or replace them? (If it replaces them, cut it.)

Remember, these are high-impact but high-risk tools. Use them only if they genuinely serve the point—not just because they seem impressive.

Visit https://clarityupconsulting.com/opk to access a companion resource hub with worksheets, prompts, and links to supporting resources like podcast episodes and articles, including videos of speakers effectively using visuals, demonstrations, and interactions.

Summary

Where you are: You understand how to support your points with visuals (that complement, never replace), demonstrations (that prove your point live), and direct interaction (that signals presence but requires confidence). You know these tools make audiences lean in—and you know they can backfire if you're not prepared.

What's in your outline: You may now have notes on a few places where you can use one or more of these tools to support certain points in your Argument, where you do or show the audience something different to just speaking and add something more. You've made sure to include these where they will have most impact.

What's next: You've built a compelling Argument—you've dismantled the Status Quo, revealed a Paradigm Shift, and supported every point with evidence and creativity. Your audience is convinced. But conviction without action is just fleeting inspiration. In Part Five, you'll learn how to create forward momentum—starting with a simple, achievable Action Step that turns belief into behavior.

PART FIVE
CREATE FORWARD MOMENTUM

Your audience is convinced. They understand the problem, they've seen why their usual approaches don't work, and they've embraced your new way of thinking.

But conviction isn't action.

The graveyard of great ideas is filled with talks that inspired people for an afternoon and were forgotten by dinner. If you want your ideas to create real change—in the audience's lives, in your industry, in the world—you need to convert belief into behavior. That's what Part Five is about: momentum.

First, you'll give them something simple to do—an Action Step they can take immediately that proves your idea works. Then you'll paint a vivid picture of the payoff, so the sacrifice feels worth it. You'll wrap up the journey with a memorable Conclusion that sticks.

As you move into this final section of your speech, the audience will feel that you're drawing to a close. You need to respect their internal sense of timing and get out before you or your ideas overstay your welcome. It's time to hand the baton to them.

The goal here isn't just to end your speech. It's to start a conversation.

20
A Simple Action Step

I'm in danger of being trampled by aspiring influencers.

We've finished day one of a major industry conference about personal branding full of high-profile speakers—influencers and multimillion-dollar business owners—and over 1,000 professionals wielding cameras, gimbals, and tiny wireless mics are heading into the lobby. I'll be speaking tomorrow and I want to get a feel for what's working for these attendees. I ask a group, "So, what were your biggest takeaways from day one?"

Over and over I get the same response. "Hm. Um… I'm not sure. It was a lot of fun. Great energy!" "I feel really inspired!" "Amped up, so good!" One attendee leaned in and practically whispered, embarrassed, "I honestly don't remember anything anyone said today. Is that bad?"

Yes, the speakers were inspiring. Energetic. Hilarious. It made for great social media moments. Pardon me, but so f***ing what? If you seek to make a real difference in the world, there's very little value in inspiration without implementation.

How to create your Action Step

You've done the hard work. You got the audience's attention, earned their engagement, and made a compelling case for adopting a new way of thinking. Now, they're looking at you and asking the most important question of all: *How do I get started?*

For some reason, this is a blind spot for many speakers. We assume that because the audience understands and fully embraces our idea, they'll naturally act on it. But that's not how behavior change works.

Give them something to do

The goal here is to give your audience something to try—as soon as possible—that will convince them that your ideas are genuinely valuable, and therefore worth spreading. Great action steps are:

- Simple
- Achievable
- Time-bound

First, they should be simple. Overwhelming your audience with a massive task will result in inaction. Think of this as a "micro action"—a small, meaningful first step that's easy to take but significant enough to create momentum.

Speakers often underestimate how complex their proposed Action Step really is. This is the curse of knowledge: the more you know about something, the harder it is to remember what it's like not to know what you know. For example, I often hear fellow human connection speakers offer an Action Step like "Each week, have a meaningful conversation with a stranger." This seems like a simple direction, but it actually involves a complex, interconnected set of skills and beliefs.

In order to "make a meaningful connection with a stranger," you need to: one, know what a meaningful conversation actually is; two, have the courage to approach a stranger; three, know a good conversation starter to get the ball rolling; and four, possess the advanced conversation skills to move from small talk to something deeper; which likely means you'll need, five, deep training and practice in reflective listening.

Whew. Not simple at all. But it also doesn't feel achievable because it's not one step, but many—each tangled up with fears and limiting beliefs. And lastly, it's something you have to keep doing over and over for an undefined amount of time, which feels like a huge commitment. One more reason not to try.

Instead, consider this Action Step: "Introduce yourself to one new person here today."

It's simple: "Just do this one thing." It's achievable: "Use one of the conversation starters I already taught you." And it's time-bound: "Do it once, before you leave the event."

Your task is to create an Action Step that people can and will take. A good rule of thumb is that if you, as an expert, think an action step is too simple, small, or obvious, it's probably perfect.

Example: How Erika got people to start even-achieving

One of the most difficult parts of Erika Coleman's talk for high achievers was the Action Step. We couldn't give the audience less to do, and we couldn't give them more to do. But we still needed them to do *something new*. We needed to create momentum.

Ultimately, Erika landed on two check-in questions, one for each type of scenario high achievers often find themselves in. I'll let Erika tell you more:

> "So, let's check in to see if we're Even-Achieving. First, let's talk about projects—work projects, home projects—something with a clear start and end date.
>
> "In this scenario, ask yourself, *If I continue at this pace, when I'm done, will I have enough energy left to celebrate?*
>
> "Let's be honest, when this project ends there will be another one and you will need to be able to pick yourself up and go again. And plus, a good celebration matters.
>
> "But of course, life doesn't always have perfect projects with obvious end dates. We all have seasons of life when things are hard, unexpected, or out of our control. If you're like me, you still want to make sure you're not leaving the people you care about behind.
>
> "So here's a check-in for this. Ask one person that you care about, 'In the last month, have I been present enough for you?'
>
> "Obviously, we hope to hear yes on both. But if not, that's okay. These aren't meant to be questions to add shame or discouragement to an already overloaded life. These are check-ins—and if they are asked regularly enough, they will

> give you the chance to recalibrate before it costs you your health or your relationships."

Each of the check-in questions is simple, achievable, and time-bound. Erika has since delivered versions of this presentation many times at various events, and she has consistently heard from attendees that they've used her questions in the days or weeks following the presentation.

More Action Step examples

Here are some additional examples of terrific Action Steps:

Dr. Yasmine Saad on making sense of negative thoughts:

> "So the next time a negative thought comes knocking at your door, resist the urge to ignore it, replace it, or reject it. Instead, decode it."

Mike Shoreman on how to keep going when life feels impossible:

> "I want you to close your eyes. Think about this: if you were crossing Lake Michigan, who would be the four people you would want to have on your team? The people who make you feel supported and cheer for you and champion you. Write down their names. Those are your four."

Dr. Ndidi Musa on how to live a significant life:

> "Sit down, write out a list of your accomplishments, and how they impacted other people. Now imagine you were reading this list about someone else. Would you think they were an impostor? Or would you think they deserved what they have?"

When you offer a simple, achievable, time-bound Action Step, your audience feels empowered rather than intimidated. They're far more likely to try it out, talk about their experience, and share your ideas with others.

How to deal with collective action

For many talks, the Action Step is straightforward, and the only thing standing in the speaker's way is their ego telling them that it's too simple. But there's a certain kind of talk that doesn't lend itself to this kind of Action Step, and those are ones discussing problems whose solutions require collective action—many people working together simultaneously to achieve something that is impossible for any one individual.

Jonathan Haidt, the famous social psychologist and author of *The Anxious Generation*,[26] is trying to create change around teen smartphone and social media use, due to its detrimental impact on mental health. Haidt acknowledges that this is a collective action problem, because you can't be the only parent who doesn't let your twelve-year-old have a smartphone. "*All* of my friends and every single kid in my grade owns a smartphone" is actually a good argument from them, because it would harm your child to ostracize them from the social group. But if you can get 50% of all parents in a school to agree to take smartphones away from their eighth graders at the same time, then you've got a real shot at change. Because, as Haidt notes, the best your kid can do then is say, "*Some* of my friends have smartphones," which isn't a compelling argument.

So when Jonathan (not a client of ours) gives keynote speeches, he has a variety of different Action Steps that help parents move toward the ultimate goal of collective action. From guides on how to get other parents on board, to The Let Grow Experience, by which parents start giving their kids opportunities to "Go do something new, on your own, unsupervised." He even offers parents a printable "Let Grow License" for the kids to keep on them at all times, in case an adult or authority figure wonders why a child is not being supervised. It has the child's name, parent's signature, and parent's phone number with this text: "I've got permission to be out here—feel free to call!"

Genius. And more importantly, doable.

Now, Jonathan Haidt is not a client, but Jane Epstein is. Jane is a survivor of sibling sexual abuse who now, in her fifties, is working to bring attention to this historically underreported and therefore understudied problem.

We built her talk delivered at TEDxBocaRaton, "Giving voice to sibling sexual abuse,"[27] not just to reach survivors but researchers, academics, and leaders who have the resources to actually work on this problem. And so we landed on this Action Step:

> "MeToo has a hashtag, and it changed the world. But where is our hashtag? Where is our support group? Well, that's up to us. So, what can we do? What can *you* do?
>
> "To those in the media, invite survivors of SSA like you do any other survivor to share their story, and normalize talking about it. If you're on the board of a school, propose an educational session for parents on the reality of SSA. Are you a social worker or a therapist? Raise awareness in conversations with your clients and colleagues."

In just sixty words, Jane offered a direct Action Step to three different kinds of people who might be watching the talk. That kind of coverage, if acted on, would create collective action.

And in fact, *People* magazine picked up the story after the video of Jane's talk started taking off, and ultimately ran a multi-page spread that debuted on the header of the home page of People.com. Jane also co-founded a nonprofit made up of parents and survivors, dedicated to spreading awareness and creating change. Her organization 5WAVES has met with policymakers and Jane has spoken on panels and delivered keynotes around the world.

That's how you create real change. That's how you make a dent in the universe.

YOUR TASK

Create your Action Step. As you do, keep this checklist in mind. It should be:

- Simple: Easy to understand
- Achievable: One thing to do, not a bundle
- Time-bound: Can be done soon

And remember, if you don't think it's too obvious or easy, it's probably not useful or simple enough.

Visit https://clarityupconsulting.com/opk to access a companion resource hub with worksheets, prompts, and links to supporting resources like podcast episodes and articles, including a worksheet on how to create your Action Step.

Summary

Where you are: You've crafted your Action Step–the simple, achievable, time-bound thing your audience can do to prove your idea works and create momentum. You know how to handle collective action problems by offering multiple pathways forward.

What's in your outline: You should now have one clear Action Step in your OPK outline—what you want the audience to do, try, or think after your speech is over.

What's next: Your audience knows what to do, but will they actually do it? There's one last barrier, and that's the perceived sacrifice. Chapter 21 shows you how to tip the Sacrifice–Stakes scale in your favor by painting a vivid picture of what becomes possible when they take action.

21

Paint A Vivid Picture Of The Payoff

We've reached the point of your talk where you've answered basically every question your audience has had:

- *Should I pay attention to this?* "Yes, it's about something you care about."
- *Does it really matter?* "Yes, something is about to go terribly wrong if you don't address it."
- *Why should I listen to you?* "I have a unique perspective you can't find anywhere else."
- *Why can't I keep doing what I've been doing?* "Those things don't work and I can prove it."

- *What's the solution, then?* "Here's a new way to think about it."
- *How do I get started?* "Just try this one, simple thing."

They know what they need to do. They just need to actually do it, and there's one thing in their way: the sacrifice (or sacrifices) it involves. *This seems like a big risk,* they'll think to themselves. What they're really asking at that moment is, *Is it really worth it?*

Sacrifices versus Stakes

I'm staring down at the empty signature line on the twentieth document that's been placed in front of me in the last hour. I look up and lock eyes with my wife, then with my attorney.

We're miserable. Our kid is miserable.

I know if I do this it will relieve our short-term pain, but it will also bring new challenges. We've already spent a year trying everything possible to avoid this monumental change. This is clearly the last option available, and all I have to do is sign my name one more time to make it happen.

My mind projects years into the future, and I imagine the freedom, the space, the room to grow. Yes, it's worth the hassle, I decide. I sign my name, take a deep breath.

"Congratulations," I hear my attorney say. "The house is yours."

Our attorney, mortgage broker, and realtor burst into cheers. I look to my right and my wife is beaming. After a year of living in a temporary apartment that we hated due to a major relocation to a new state, we are finally homeowners again.

There are so many reasons not to change, and everyone weighs the sacrifices before taking action. The Sacrifice–Stakes scale is simple. If the sacrifices are heavier than the stakes, the person won't take action. If the stakes are heavier than the sacrifices, they will.

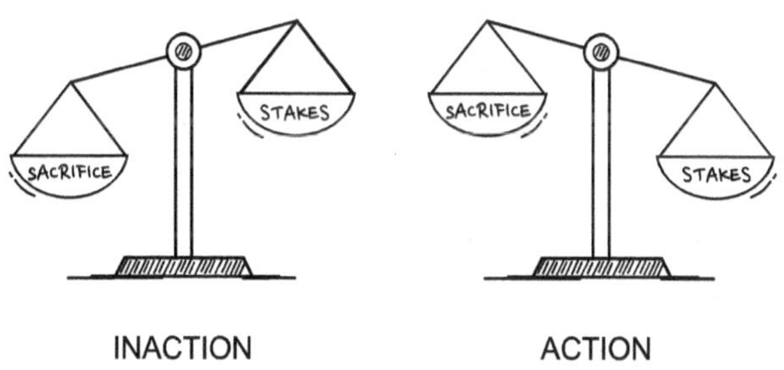

The Sacrifice–Stakes scale

Right before signing the closing documents on our house, I thought about everything I was going to sacrifice:

- Savings, in the form of a down payment and closing costs (which comes with both tangible sacrifice [money—lots of it] and intangible (feelings of financial security).
- Stability, in the form of moving for the second time in twelve months, which as most of us know, is a tremendous investment of time and energy (oh, and more money).
- Routine, in the form of new grocery stores, new driving routes, new neighbors, and importantly, a new school for my kid.

It doesn't matter how hard things are. If change feels worse, we don't budge. The "devil you know" and all that.

So, what pushed me over the edge in order to take action and sign the damn thing? Well, I imagined the long-term, positive results. The sweeping, epic climax of the movie. The pot of gold at the end of the rainbow.

My thoughts went to my son, Milo, getting to run and jump around the house without having to constantly tell him to be quiet or stop having fun (for fear of neighbors complaining to the leasing office); to having a backyard where he can play and explore; a safe community for going on walks and riding bikes; a house large enough to host friends and family, and room for me and my wife, Lindsey, to each have home offices. As I imagined that possible future, the Stakes–Sacrifice scale tipped away from the sacrifices.

Like everything else we've discussed, we aren't just going to hope that your audience will do this thinking for themselves. We're going to intentionally guide them through the exercise, so that they can take action and change their lives for the better.

Help them picture the payoff

Back in Chapter 6 we identified your audience's primary fear and its opposite. In Erika Coleman's case, her audience of high achievers is afraid of letting people down, and so they are feeling insecure. We therefore decided that by the end of her talk the audience should feel a sense of security. This feeling of security is what success looks like for them—the payoff for taking action.

Erika went with a simple, understated Success section:

> "If [these Action Step questions] are asked regularly enough, they will give you the chance to recalibrate before it costs you your health or your relationships.

> "True champions will pace themselves, so they have the energy to celebrate their own success and the presence to cheer their teammates on as well."

Not giving your all is hard for high achievers, and can feel like a great sacrifice. So Erika weighs this against what it means to be a true champion.

It's not enough to give your audience an Action Step. They need to believe it's worth the discomfort of trying, so don't leave them guessing. Show them what could be waiting on the other side. Make it vivid, but not exaggerated. Honest, but aspirational. Describe what life could look like if they take the action. What would they notice? What would change in their day-to-day experience? What might someone else observe about them?

Your job here is not to promise an outcome, but to make one feel possible. Here are three ways to do it.

1. Show success with a case study

One of the most effective ways to paint this picture is with a short case study. The story should center on a person who was once in the audience's shoes. They had the same problem. They made the same shift. They took the step you're now recommending. And they ended up somewhere wonderful.

Dr. Margaret Rutherford—who speaks about depression that is masked by perfectionism and why we need to normalize talking about suicidal thoughts—followed her Action Step with this short case study:

> "A man—let's call him Michael—who was internationally prominent in his field, came into therapy, laughing that no one would ever imagine him doing so. He'd grown up in a family where talking about feelings, especially painful ones, wasn't allowed. But recently, his father had died suddenly. And he'd never told his dad he loved him, despite the tumultuous relationship they'd had. His lack of action seemed unforgivable.
>
> "As we talked about everything from his childhood to current decisions he was trying to make, he began to see patterns. He'd always covered up how abusive his childhood had been, how he'd turned greater and greater accomplishments into destinations that he'd hoped would blot out or blur pain that he kept deep inside, hidden away. But the plan hadn't worked. And in one session, he revealed, very painfully, that he'd had moments of considering taking his own life. I told him that was normal, given the extent of his pain.
>
> "Through our work, he learned to have compassion for not only himself as a child, and in some ways his father, but not to carry shame that was not his to carry. He could feel sadness

> and grief, without pummeling himself with self-loathing. And he decided to keep living. I'll never forget his smile as he walked in one day and told me about his most recent airplane trip.
>
> "He said, 'Not only was I journaling rather than working, writing about my memories and feelings, in public. But when I felt a tear roll down my face, I didn't care.'"

Quiet, beautiful, and compelling. A great case study and a clear image of Success.

2. Promise a return on investment

But hey, maybe you've already told a lot of stories in your talk, or you don't have one perfect case study that exactly captures everything you've talked about (life is rarely as perfect as our speeches). In that case, you might consider simply listing the common benefits or primary outcome when someone takes action on your idea.

Toward the end of my keynote on human connection, I tell the audience:

> "You can create a culture of connection. But more importantly, you can *become* a culture of connection. When we ask meaningful questions and listen to understand, we make the people around us feel heard, understood, and valued. And then, one person at a time, incremental

> change creates revolution. And we are in desperate, desperate need of a human connection revolution right now. And we need *you* to lead it. Because if not you, who's going to do it?"

Yes, it tilts motivational. But it also paints a picture of what you get in exchange for making a better effort to connect with others on a daily basis.

3. Describe an imagined future

But what if you're dealing in cutting edge research, science that's on the brink of innovation, and you don't actually know for sure what's going to happen if we implement these ideas? Then give us an imagined future; paint a picture of what might happen, within reason, based on what you currently understand, amplified by your expertise.

That's what Dr. Jacob Levenson did after proposing that scientists adopt Time of Arrival technology as the future of animal tracking:

> "And now, imagine if ToA was everywhere. With smaller tags we can now expand to include so many more species and life stages previously too small to carry tags safely.
>
> "For example, we don't really know where sea turtles go from the time they hatch and crawl down a beach, to years later when they return to nest. These fifteen to twenty years are known

> as the lost years. Smaller tags, weighing just a gram or two, can uncover these mysteries. But ToA goes way beyond my work in animal tracking.
>
> "Smaller and more affordable tags also have significant implications for public safety. Imagine if every life jacket on a ship was equipped with a nickel-sized tracking tag, creating a global network similar to Apple AirTags, but without the need for proximity to a cellphone."

Jake is tipping the scales in his favor, by strongly weighing the possible benefits of ToA against the hassle and anxiety of adopting a totally new technology. Plus, he moves the benefits beyond his own field to the broader public interest, amplifying the potential upside and squashing the sacrifices.

YOUR TASK

Jot down a handful of ways that things might reasonably get better if someone does what you're asking them to do in the Action Step. How will taking action on your speech improve their life? Their work? The lives of others, their community, or the world?

Then think about the best way to make sure they really *feel* it. Should you show them a case study? Describe an imagined future? Or show them how and why those pesky sacrifices will be worth it, because the return on investment will eclipse all downside. Highlight the specific benefits or changes they'll experience.

This should be vivid but honest; aspirational without exaggeration. Once you've decided, write this in the Success section of your OPK outline.

Visit https://clarityupconsulting.com/opk to access a companion resource hub with worksheets, prompts, and links to supporting resources like podcast episodes and articles, including one I authored on the Sacrifice–Stakes scale.

Summary

Where you are: You understand how to tip the Sacrifice–Stakes scale by making the payoff feel real and attainable. You've chosen your approach: a case study (someone who was in their shoes and succeeded), return on investment (listing the benefits), or imagined future (what becomes possible based on your expertise). You know how to make the upside feel impossible to ignore.

What's in your outline: In your OPK outline, you now have a vivid, aspirational image of the future that's possible for your audience if they take the Action Step you've proposed. This section should only take a minute or so in most speeches, and no more than three minutes in long keynotes. You're not proving anything new here, you're helping the audience feel what's possible.

What's next: You've delivered a complete Argument. You've made your case; your audience knows what to do and is ready to act. But in twenty-four hours, they'll forget what you said—unless you cement it in their memory with a Conclusion that sticks. Chapter 22 teaches you how to deliver a Mic-Drop moment that ensures your core message stays with them long after the applause.

22 Conclude With A Mic-Drop

Okay, this is it. The final question on every audience member's mind.

By the time you finish the Success portion of the speech, they can feel it. This talk is over. Pay attention on stage and you'll know precisely the moment the audience is ready for the speech to end. One person uncrosses their legs. A few others check the time. One glances at the exit. Not because you've lost them (hopefully), but because you've done your job and they're itching to do something about what they've learned.

You're in the window of opportunity, and this window does not stay open long. If you keep talking after that moment has passed with another five minutes of content—one more example, an extra lesson, a long string of thank yous—you lose some of the goodwill you've built, and possibly all the magic. The best speeches end at the peak of clarity and connection.

Great Conclusions are fast and effortless

A strong Conclusion needs only two things:

1. Deliver the core message
2. Leave them with a memorable mic-drop

You can do both in under ninety seconds. Anything more risks stealing attention from the thing you want to leave them with. Way back in Chapter 7 we created our one-sentence filter statement. This is the moment to return to that statement, because as your North Star, it can also serve as the core message for your audience. The throughline. The one thing that underlines the entire talk.

First though, let's spend some time crafting your Mic-Drop, then we'll put it all together to create a killer Conclusion.

Craft your Mic-Drop

As they're eagerly awaiting the moment you finally shut up, your audience will ask themselves one last, critical question: *Wait, what was this all about again?*

Yep, that's right. They forgot already. Well, not quite—but they will, if you don't cement it in their brain. That's why we're going to lean hard into recency bias: we tend to remember the most recent thing we heard or experienced more deeply than anything else.

So your final line is what they'll walk out thinking about. The literal last thing you say should be the thing you want them to remember and repeat. But it can be incredibly daunting to come up with a single sentence that does all the work of summing up your speech. That's why I use the Billboard Prompt.

The Billboard Prompt

If you only had the space of a billboard to deliver a single message to everyone in the world you're trying to reach, change, or impact, what would that message say?

Remember, you don't have a lot of characters. The smaller the text, the harder it is to read. And people are driving fast, so they've just got a second or two. What is that line? What's the one thing that you want everyone to know, even if they didn't know anything else about your work? Write it down next to the core message you pulled in from earlier.

Now, let's creatively put these elements together to produce your conclusion.

Craft your Conclusion

Conclusions are more of an art than a science, so I'm not going to offer you a structure for putting it together. Goodness knows I've given enough structure in this book. Instead, I'll let you borrow inspiration from some of my favorite Conclusions we've worked on.

Erika Coleman

Talk: "How to reduce stress without sacrificing success."

Conclusion: "Remember, we don't have to give our all to give our best. In fact, we shouldn't. We can't. True champions will pace themselves, so they have the energy to celebrate their own success and the presence to cheer their teammates on as well. I believe everyone deserves the chance to reach for success without drowning in stress. And that's the art of even-achieving."

Erika delivered her talk at TEDxOneonta in October 2025. I flew to upstate New York to attend the filming live, and it was spectacular. She has since delivered versions of this speech many times, and it gets better with each variation.

Dr. Carole Blueweiss

Talk: "Your socks may hold the key to aging better."

Conclusion: "So stand on one leg every day and try putting on your socks. Challenge yourself. Build better balance, and the last years of your life may just be the best years of your life."

Dr. Marjorie Aunos

Talk: "What we can learn from parents with disabilities."

Conclusion: "As parents, we do the best we can, with what we have. So next time you see a parent, in your community or on TikTok—don't judge them too harshly. But do ask yourself, which creative solutions are they using right now? And if you come across a parent with a disability, don't focus on what they don't have that you do, but rather focus on what they do have that you don't. And maybe *they* can teach *you* something new."

Carey Theil and Christine Dorchak

Talk: "How to be an activist who creates real change."[28]

Conclusion: "Over the course of the last twenty-five years, we have learned many lessons for successful activism. First, that you must be willing to persist through failure and even let it fuel you. Second, that you can't just change minds, you also must change the law. And finally, the lesson that was most essential of all: successful activism is a marathon, not a sprint.

"It's hard to imagine that a spotted dog would become the inspiration for a worldwide fight. That the campaign would end greyhound racing. And that after a decade of suffering, that same dog would come home to us. And yet, it happened. It proved to us that politics can still be a force for good. And it's still possible to change the world."

Dr. Jacob Levenson

Talk: "The surprising ways space technology will save our oceans."

Conclusion: "Eight years ago, I was stuck in traffic with a question: could we use space technology to track animals? Now, we're doing more than tracking—we're changing how we protect the ocean, its inhabitants, and everyone who shares this planet. The ocean never stands still. But with the right technology, we can move with it."

Peder Tellefsdal

Talk: "How to seek forgiveness when relationships are on the line."

Conclusion: "We need to reclaim the words to describe the inner struggle between good and evil that we all experience. We need to focus less on what we say and more on what we do. And by using the language and practicing it, you open the door to the most valuable of all human experiences: grace. Own your screw-ups. Ask for forgiveness. Go all in."

The most important thing is to end when the speech is done. Your Conclusion doesn't need to be clever or poetic, but it does need to feel earned. Most importantly, just say the thing. Then stop talking.

Whatever you do, don't trail into "I hope this was helpful," or "I'll be at the back of the room in case..."

Stop. Just end it. Say "thank you" if you wish, then take your bow. Wave. Smile. Then leave the stage and let the audience pick up the conversation from there.

YOUR TASK

Build your Conclusion by combining your Core Message and a Mic-Drop moment. Under "Conclusion" in your OPK outline, write:

- Core Message: Your filter statement or main throughline
- Mic-Drop: Your Billboard Prompt answer—the one line that sums up everything

Then, practice saying it out loud. After your Mic-Drop, you will say "Thank you," pause, and then leave the stage. Nothing more.

Visit https://clarityupconsulting.com/opk to access a companion resource hub with worksheets, prompts, and links to supporting resources like podcast episodes and articles. You can also watch all the talks I've quoted in the examples above, to fully appreciate the power of their Conclusions.

Summary

Where you are: You've crafted your conclusion—a reinforcement of your core message paired with a memorable Mic-Drop line. You understand that great conclusions are fast (under ninety seconds), earned (not clever for clever's sake), and final (no trailing "I hope this was helpful" nonsense). The recency bias is your friend—your last line is what they'll remember and repeat.

What's in your outline: You now have a full speech outlined. The rest is style and flair; all the substance is now here in your completed OPK outline.

What's next: You've built the complete structure of your keynote, from opening to conclusion. But a well-structured talk can still fall flat without the magical touches that create momentum and keep audiences engaged throughout. Part Six teaches you the advanced techniques that transform a good speech into an unforgettable experience: signposting, open loops, callbacks, and the minimum viable performance skills you actually need.

PART SIX
ELEVATE YOUR SPEECH

Design beats delivery, every time.

I stand by that principle as I've watched it play out again and again, from the nerdiest of scientists to the driest executives. Anybody can give a compelling keynote speech that captures attention, earns engagement, and ultimately creates lasting change... if it's well designed.

And right now, you're capable of designing a speech in the top 10% of those your audience has ever seen. That, in and of itself, is a Herculean feat—and you should be proud of how far you've come.

Having said that, audiences appreciate style.

In this final section we're going to discover a handful of ways to elevate your keynote from a compelling script to a captivating talk.

Chapter 23 will teach you three advanced speech design tactics to increase the likelihood of engagement across the entire talk. These are particularly useful for longer presentations when attention spans can dip regardless of how well designed the talk or charismatic a speaker you are.

Then in Chapter 24 I'll give you a crash course on performance techniques that have the highest effort-to-result ratio. We're not talking Atomic Habits here; we're talking the Pareto Principle: 20% of your effort for 80% of the results.

Let's elevate your speech.

23

Add Magical Touch Points To The Journey

If you've built your keynote according to the structure in this book, at this point you'rc in great shape. Like, way better than most. Your speech is probably already in the top 10% and, for most, that's more than enough.

But if you're like me, who in eighth grade was reduced to tears because I got a 107% on a math test when it was possible to get 108%, then this chapter is for you. What follows are three speech elements that you really only see from top communicators—the folks in the top 1%. These are a plan, signposting, and open loops.

Using any of these techniques will give your speech an immediate jolt of professionalism and polish.

The Plan

When Milo was a toddler, I would often pick him up from daycare and then rush through the grocery store desperately looking for something to make for dinner. Not for Milo (he ate the same three foods all toddlers eat), but for me and my wife. Carrying a toddler through a grocery store at 5 p.m. is no easy feat. Combined with the lack of sleep and an urgent hunger, I had to move as fast as possible.

And so I'd often find myself in the frozen food section, staring at a wall of frozen pizzas—yes, I know how unhealthy they are. One time, as my eyes started glazing over, a particular pizza box came into focus. It had three large yellow circles, each containing a number (one, two or three). Next to each number were just a few words:

1. "Remove pizza from wrapping."
2. "Bake at 400° for 16 minutes."
3. "Enjoy your pizza."

Remove pizza. Bake pizza. Enjoy pizza. *I can do that.*

Sold.

People love a plan

Telling the audience your plan tells them you have a plan. It gives them the confidence that you've thought this through, that you're not just winging it—and with confidence comes trust. And yet I rarely see a speaker explicitly lay out a plan, roadmap, or agenda for their presentation.

But what goes in The Plan? I recommend three steps in a perfect world, four at most. And you create your plan *after* you've designed the speech. That way, you simply have to look at what you're going to cover and break it into three or four steps.

For example, in my signature speech on human connection I lay out this plan for the talk they're about to hear:

1. What is human connection?
2. How to read people's minds.
3. Connection in practice.

I lay them out on a single slide, and with each step I offer one sentence of explanation:

> "First, we're going to discuss the definition of human connection. Because if we don't know what it is, it's almost impossible to achieve it. Second, I'm going to teach you how to read people's minds. Because if you knew what people were thinking, it would be way easier to connect with them, wouldn't it? And finally, connection in practice. I'll give you three

> specific, tactical ways to make quick, meaningful connections with anyone, in any situation."

And just like that, the audience knows that they're in good hands. Bonus points if you return to The Plan through the speech, to remind the audience where they've been, where they are, and where they're going. Which brings me to signposting.

Signposting

As we discussed back in Chapter 1 on the Eight Questions, no matter how well-structured your talk is, your audience only experiences it in real-time. There are no chapter headings. No progress bar. No rewind. If they lose track of where they are in the Argument, even briefly, you've lost them. And make no mistake: people will lose track of where they are—because a notification popped up, a door slammed, or simply because their mind went off on a tangent related to something you said. Whatever the reason, when they snap back into focus, they might not know "where they are" in the speech anymore. This is why signposting matters.

Signposting is a verbal cue that tells the audience where they are in your talk. It helps them track progress, understand transitions, and stay with you from one idea to the next. Signposts aren't necessarily formal labels or slide titles. They're often ordinary phrases, spoken with intention. They sound like:

- "So, why did I tell you that?"
- "That's the first belief. Let's move to the second."
- "Here's where a pattern emerges."
- "Let's talk about what happens if we actually do this."
- "But the next question I asked myself was..."
- "So, what's the takeaway? What do we learn from that?"

Most speakers don't include phrases like this and instead barrel on from one idea to the next assuming the audience is fully with them at all times. Especially in the Status Quo section, where you may be addressing three or four distinct beliefs, signposting is essential. A quick reminder like, "That's belief number two," is often enough to keep the structure clear.

I recommend adding signposts *after* you've already built your argument. Go back through and look at the transitions between major points. Then, for each one, add a sentence that tells the audience what's happening next.

If you ever find yourself wondering why the audience seems to disengage halfway through a section, even when your content is strong, adequate signposting is one of the first things to check for. But if you *really* want people to stay engaged, your unfair advantage comes from an open loop.

Open loops

In my TEDx talk I told a story about performing magic for an older gentleman and his wife, only to realize too late that he was blind. When I wrote the talk, something in my gut told me not to finish the story right away. I waited until the end to reveal how Ed could "see" the cards, despite being blind.

That instinct turned out to be right. In doing so, I stumbled upon the technique of withholding information until later in the talk. It's possible that this one decision alone transformed my talk from good to potentially viral.

What is an open loop? An open loop is an unfinished thread. It's a story you start but don't finish. A question you raise but don't answer. A moment you hold without resolving.

That tension buys attention.

The audience will naturally stay engaged with you because they don't know when you're going to close the loop, and they don't want to miss it. But there's a fine line between magic and manipulation with this technique. If you're going to use an open loop, there are some important considerations.

How to use an open loop without losing the audience

First, the audience must genuinely want the answer to this question, or the resolution to this story. As fans of the 2010s TV show *Lost* will tell you, a "mystery box" is only as good as what's inside it. If you string the audience along and then deliver an unsatisfying or merely perfunctory conclusion to the open loop, they'll resent you for wasting their time and attention.

Second, you must close the loop within a reasonable amount of time. No matter how curious the audience is about the resolution to your story, if enough time passes, they'll stop caring. Partly because they've moved on to caring about something else in your speech, and partly because they've simply forgotten the setup.

How long is that? I have no idea. It seems to vary from speaker to speaker, topic to topic, audience to audience, and open loop to open loop. Think of it like a balloon: the longer you blow it up, the bigger the pop has to be. No one wants a long setup followed by a weak payoff. My rule of thumb is that there should be absolutely no longer than thirty minutes between the opening and closing of the loop. More experienced speakers can get away with being on the longer end of that spectrum; novices should go for a maximum of ten minutes between opening and closing.

And most importantly, you absolutely cannot forget to close the loop. Unless you wish to incur the wrath of 200 sweaty fifteen-year-olds, as I did once in the gymnasium of a youth summer camp when I ended my speech and walked off while dozens of kids screamed, "Wait, but how did the blind guy see the cards?" Thankfully, my event hosts let me hop back on stage and close the loop properly and I got to spend five extra minutes finishing the story. This was a solid reminder that open loops are powerful. And like all powerful tools, they need to be handled with care.

These are the magic moments that take a strong talk and make it extraordinary. Now it's your turn.

YOUR TASK

If you want to make your talk sparkle, review your OPK to see where you can incorporate these level-up tools:

1. **Write your plan:** What are the steps your talk covers? Write them out as a roadmap for your audience, with a one-sentence explanation—then say them out loud early in your talk.
2. **Add signposting phrases:** Look at the transitions between major sections of your speech. Can you add one sentence before each to orient your audience in their journey? Use phrases like "That's the first belief, let's move to the second."

3. **Introduce one open loop:** Choose a story or question you can start but not finish right away. Where will you return to it? Make sure the payoff is worth the wait.

Not every keynote needs all of these advanced techniques, but knowing they exist and how to use them is part of what separates the best from the rest. If you've managed to incorporate any of these into your speech, welcome to the top 1%.

Visit https://clarityupconsulting.com/opk to access a companion resource hub with worksheets, prompts, and links to supporting resources like podcast episodes and articles.

Summary

Where you are: You understand three advanced techniques that separate the top 1% of speeches from the rest—The Plan (a three- to four-step roadmap), signposting (verbal cues that orient the audience), and open loops (unfinished threads that create tension). These aren't required, but they take a talk to the next level.

What's in your outline: In your complete OPK outline you may have added one or more of these elements:

- The Plan (near the beginning, after your opening)
- Signposting (at transitions between major points)
- Open loop (where it's opened and closed)

What's next: You've built a complete, polished keynote using the OPK structure. The speech itself is done. But you still need to deliver it, and that means stepping on stage with confidence. Chapter 24 gives you the minimum viable performance skills you need: not how to be a professional performer, but how to avoid undermining your excellent content with distracting delivery habits.

24
Crash Course On Performance

I've just completed the soundcheck in a freezing, early morning banquet hall. One hour from now the elegant white and gold tables will be full of executives and top-level leaders from across the accounting industry—and I'm set to deliver the kick-off keynote on human connection.

"Brian, this is Tom. He represents the top sponsor for today. We're going to give him a few minutes to speak before you go on."

Tom is well dressed and self-assured. Unlike many experts who've been asked to speak, he doesn't seem nervous at all.

"Good to meet you, Tom. You do this a lot?"

"Oh yeah," he smiles broadly. "We sponsor hundreds of events like this, and I give this talk at every one of them. I've given it hundreds of times."

As the room fills, I mingle, introducing myself and getting a read on the pulse of the audience. There's a lot of energy, excitement, and anticipation. This group is eager to engage.

The president of the association introduces Tom, whose company makes a piece of innovative accounting technology. He takes the stage and begins talking. I scan the room and notice that everyone is leaning in. Even the back row put their phones away. Whatever Tom's technology does is clearly very important to these people.

But then, something happens. Tom starts reading from pages and pages of typed script in a monotone. Randomly he veers off on a tangent, making side comments and attempts at humor that don't land. His slides are so packed with text they're incomprehensible. Folks start leaning back into their seats. A few phones come back out, and then more. By the time Tom wraps up, hardly anyone is even looking up. His final slide has a QR code, offering a trial run of free access to the software, and only three people in the entire room scan it.

Tom's company paid thousands of dollars in event sponsorship to ensure their product reached a room of over 200 top leaders and economic decision-makers in their target market—people who were eager to listen to him talk about a product that could genuinely help them. They could have bought from him, invested in his company, or referred his work to others. It was a golden opportunity, and he wasted it.

Delivery matters (a little)

I suppose a book on writing speeches wouldn't be complete without at least a sideways glance to the act of delivering those words in front of an audience. Now, I stand by the thesis of this book: you *can* deliver a world-class keynote speech that moves people to action, no charisma or performance chops required. Still, a little bit of performance goes a long way to making a message sing.

These are the quick tips I offer all our clients before they take the stage, things that work particularly well for otherwise untrained speakers who don't have time to become masterful performers.

Speak with one person at a time

If you're trying to "project to the back of the room" you're going to end up shouting at the audience. Likewise, if you're constantly scanning the room in an effort to make everyone feel included, no one will.

Instead, find one person in the audience, someone you can lock eyes with, and deliver this line, or the next two lines, just for them. Speak as if you were sitting across from them having coffee and let the microphone do the work of amplifying your voice to the whole crowd. Then find someone else and deliver the next couple of lines to them. And so on.

This approach will ground you in a conversational tone that feels warm and inviting, and that direct connection you make with one person will carry through the rest of the audience. It will even carry through the cameras and into the future for folks watching on a replay. Leave theatrics to the actors and simply chat with the audience, one person at a time.

Use the stage but don't wander

Whatever space you have, consider using it. There are so many opportunities to engage the audience visually and emotionally with movement, and yet so many speakers stand in one place the entire time they're on stage. Physical movement creates energy, for you and the audience. So use the space.

However—and this a big however—if you find yourself moving without a reason, stop. What I mean is, many untrained speakers have a habit of aimlessly meandering around the stage, shifting their weight, moving from here to there, switching which hand the mic is in, turning around and staring at their slides… Movement creates energy, but that energy is only good if it's purposeful. If you're telling a story that involves action, excitement, or momentum, then physically moving from one side of the stage to the other while you tell it can add to that feeling.

You can, for example, choose to always tell stories from an imaginary spot on the left side of the stage, but only deliver data from an imaginary spot on the right, subconsciously anchoring the audience, so they know what type of content they should expect at different parts of the presentation.

Finally, if at all possible, avoid or get out from behind the podium. Podiums obscure most of your body, literally creating a barrier between you and the audience. That robs you of the ability to physically engage with hand gestures or movement, and encourages reading from notes. All of which are mojo killers.

Do a dress rehearsal

What non-professional speakers don't realize about a dress rehearsal is that it's not for actually rehearsing the speech. You should have that locked down way before this moment.

Instead, this is your chance to get comfortable with the stage, the microphone, the room. Make sure you insist on, and use, a dress rehearsal. Walk around the stage and feel it under your feet. Is it hard? Does it give? Is there a throw rug that nobody taped down you might trip on and smash your face? (This has definitely never happened to me.)

As well as the stage, get familiar with the tech. How does the mic sound? Headsets, lavaliers, and handhelds all sound different—and they feel different to use. Does the microphone react to dynamics? If you get loud, does it also get loud with you, or do you feel it squashing down your volume? How well can you hear yourself? Many venues don't have monitors (speakers on the floor pointed toward you on stage), so you can't tell what you actually sound like to the audience. If it's the perfect volume in the seats but you can't hear yourself, you may instinctively talk louder to try to compensate, which will cause the audience to feel like you're yelling.

Gain perspective. Sit in the audience while other speakers rehearse to get a sense of the audience's vantage. Sit in the front row. What does it look and sound like? Then sit at the back of the room. Then the middle, off to one side. Notice how your perception of the presenter changes. Are there any creaky doors or street noise coming through the walls that might distract you?

Where will you walk on from, and how long does it take to get from backstage or your seat to the spot where you'll be speaking? Count your steps if you like and plan which foot to start walking from so that you land on the spot comfortably and don't have to awkwardly shuffle around to find your place.

Speaking is stressful enough. Eliminate all possible surprises by understanding as much of the environment as you can before taking the stage.

Memorize the key moments

You could, in theory, memorize the entire keynote. Broadway actors memorize three hours of lines somebody else wrote, so surely you can memorize a twenty-minute talk consisting of your own words. You can, but you don't have to.

Instead, focus on a handful of key moments that you want to nail. These should include your opening, your Mic-Drop final sentence, your Story Hook, and the one-line Paradigm Shift. You might also consider memorizing transition lines that move you from one part of the speech into the next. Having key moments down cold ensures that even if you get a little lost, or veer off into an unexpected anecdote, you can always find your way back to the talk you planned on giving, with confidence and authority.

If nothing else, memorize your opening. When you walk out on stage and nail the opening, you'll give yourself a huge boost of confidence that settles your body and in turn makes the audience feel like they're in good hands, so they also relax.

Begin at the beginning

Speaking of your opening, there are so many ways speakers botch the introduction. These are the big ones:

- **Saying hello:** Starting with "Hello, everyone" might seem polite, but it wastes precious seconds without adding value. The audience already knows you're there. They need to know why they should pay attention.
- **Thanking the organizer:** While it's courteous to thank the event organizer, doing so as your first words distracts from the audience's focus, and bursts the bubble of anticipation for your talk. Save your gratitude for later, after you've established your message and connection with the crowd. I thank organizers and the A/V (if applicable) just before my conclusion.
- **Banter with the audience:** Casual comments like "Wow, what a great crowd!" or "I hope you're all awake after that lunch!" might feel like icebreakers, but they often fall flat. Banter wastes time and risks alienating your audience if it doesn't land perfectly. And again, it doesn't add any value.
- **Offering credentials:** Launching into your bio or achievements at the start might feel necessary to build credibility, but it's a momentum killer—and it reeks of insecurity. You're on stage, in a

spotlight, and holding a microphone for a reason. You will prove that you are a trustworthy guide once the audience is actually engaged in the speech.

- **Preamble:** And lastly, I never, ever, *ever* want to hear the words, "Before I begin…" come out of your mouth.

Say it with me: you cannot begin before you begin. If there's something so important that you need to say it before you start your speech, you have just admitted to the audience that your speech is poorly designed.

Don't do it. I'll know, and I'll haunt you.

Focus on the message

My experience working with experts who are not trained or practiced in public speaking is that they become more comfortable on stage and deliver better performances when they're convinced that the content is good. That the right ideas are in the right order, and it's going to land the way they want.

The One-Page Keynote framework is precisely designed to give you that confidence. If you have something real to offer, and you get it into a structure that answers the questions the audience is already asking, in the order they're asking them, you will be more relaxed on stage and will deliver a better performance. And the more times you do it, the more comfortable you'll get experimenting with movement, breath, dynamics, and all the fun performance elements that traditional speaker coaches spend most of their time focusing on.

Lead with message design, and the performance will follow.

Visit https://clarityupconsulting.com/opk to access a companion resource hub with worksheets, prompts, and links to supporting resources like podcast episodes and articles, a Dress Rehearsal Checklist, and an in-depth article I co-authored with Francisco Mahfuz and Ioana Jongsma on how to memorize speeches.

Conclusion: It's Time To Restore Humanity's Faith In Experts

Speaking is an honor. It is a rare and special privilege. And people know that. Whether it's a room of 20, 200, or 2,000, everyone in the seats assumes that you have earned the right to their attention. You must have done *something* noteworthy, innovative, or at least interesting to deserve an unbroken allotment of precious time where everybody is 100% focused on you. Yet most speakers undermine this privileged position by delivering speeches that are unworthy of our attention, let alone our engagement.

This will not happen to you.

You now have a complete system for designing keynotes that move people to action, no charisma required.

In Part One, you learned that great speeches aren't about charisma or performance—they're about structure. You discovered the eight questions every audience is silently asking, and the One-Page Keynote framework that answers them in the right order. You chose your audience, your topic, and your angle.

In Part Two, you learned how to grab attention by meeting the audience where they are. You identified their known want and the core problem standing in their way. You dug into their fears and beliefs—the internal forces driving their behavior. And you created a Filter statement to keep you on message throughout.

In Part Three, you learned how to earn engagement in the critical first minutes of your talk. You explored three classic ways to open, learned when to simply state the Premise, established the Stakes, framed your talk with a Core Question, and chose the right story to qualify yourself as a trustworthy guide.

In Part Four, you learned how to make your case. You took a tour through the Status Quo and dismantled it with empathy. You revealed a Paradigm Shift that changes how your audience thinks about the problem. You chose a structure for your Argument and learned how to support each point with data, stories, metaphors, and demonstrations.

In Part Five, you learned how to create forward momentum. You gave your audience a simple Action

Step. You painted a vivid picture of Success. You concluded with a Mic-Drop.

Finally, in Part Six you added the magical touch points—plans, signposts, open loops—that separate good talks from world-class speeches, and learned a handful of performance elements to take your script from the page to the stage.

That's the system. It works for TED-style talks, twenty-minute presentations, and sixty-minute keynotes. It works for scientists and executives, and activists and entrepreneurs. It works whether you're a natural performer or terrified of the spotlight. Because design beats delivery, every time. But I have a confession…

This book isn't really about designing keynote speeches. It's about something much deeper, and much more important than any one speech.

The death of expertise

We are living in a world in which true experts, specialists, and industry leaders are dismissed and derided as "gatekeepers." In a time when an amateur blog post, podcast, or influencer's take is often seen as more trustworthy than credentialed or institutional knowledge. We are in a trust recession and experiencing a widespread backlash against expertise of all kinds.

But there's still a place for specialized knowledge, legitimate expertise, and mission-driven leadership.

Experts aren't always right—but they're more likely to be. You understand your topic in a way most people never will. You see the nuance, the risks, and the potential. What you know could change lives, maybe even shape the future of your field—or the world. But none of that matters unless you earn buy-in from the people who matter. We defeat bad ideas not with great ideas, but by making a better case for good ideas.

If you know something important, something that would make people's lives or the world better, then you have a moral obligation to communicate it clearly. Not a professional obligation. A *moral* obligation. It is your responsibility. Your duty. Your imperative. Because ideas don't speak for themselves—people do.

So speak up for your ideas.

Notes

1 B Miller, "How to magically connect with anyone" (TEDxManchesterHighSchool, June 17, 2015), www.youtube.com/watch?v=D4cV8yfgNyI, accessed January 28, 2026

2 As relayed by Julian Treasure during a 2025 interview with Chris Duffy for TED: TED, "5x TED speaker gives you communication advice: Julian Treasure: How to be a better human" (October 15, 2025), https://youtu.be/SuaxadRqJpM?si=foP0BGFqPxEn3kx6, accessed January 12, 2026

3 B Kennedy and A Tyson, "Americans' trust in scientists, positive views of science continue to decline" (Pew Research Center,

November 14, 2023), www.pewresearch.org/science/2023/11/14/americans-trust-in-scientists-positive-views-of-science-continue-to-decline, accessed 18 December 18, 2025

4 C Deane, "Americans' deepening mistrust of institutions" (The Pew Charitable Trusts, October 17, 2024), www.pew.org/en/trend/archive/fall-2024/americans-deepening-mistrust-of-institutions, accessed December 18, 2025

5 L Silver, S Keeter, S Kramer, J Lippert, S Hernandez Ramones, A Cooperman, C Baronavski, B Webster, R Nadeem, and J Chavda, "Americans' trust in one another" (Pew Research Center, May 8, 2025), www.pewresearch.org/2025/05/08/americans-trust-in-one-another, accessed December 18, 2025

6 E Coleman, "How to reduce stress without sacrificing success" (TEDxOneonta, October 4, 2025), https://youtu.be/9y1ZTgBClVI?si=zOe8_UaRu02PFtFo, accessed February 11, 2026

7 B Miller, "How to get people to listen to you" (March 2, 2020), https://youtu.be/BBZ_VEDtYgM, accessed January 1, 2026

8 It's worth noting that trying to shatter a mistaken or misguided belief is usually a fool's errand. It's unlikely you'll convince someone that their deeply held assumption is wrong from the front of the room. My colleague Tamsen Webster argues that instead we should aim to replace a mistaken or misguided belief with a

stronger one. More on that in her book *Say What They Can't Unhear* (Page Two, 2024).

9 I first encountered the roots of this framework in Jeremey Donovan's book *How to Deliver a TED Talk* (McGraw-Hill, 2013), which I read while preparing for my own TEDx talk. In the chapter on "Choosing an Idea Worth Spreading," Donovan writes: "While there is no single best way to phrase your idea worth spreading during your talk, there is an excellent way to think about it during the planning stages. To impose good discipline, the format I recommend is 'To (action) so that (outcome).'" Donovan provides several examples from successful TED and TEDx talks but does not develop the concept further. It was the most practically useful idea in the book, and I have spent the past decade building on it, stress-testing it, and turning it into a repeatable clarity tool. Hat tip to Mr. Donovan.

10 C Blueweiss, "Your socks may hold the key to aging better" (TEDxBocaRaton, June 6, 2024), www.youtube.com/watch?v=6F6m9CGFnk0, accessed December 19, 2025

11 P Tellefsdal, "How to seek forgiveness when relationships are on the line" (TEDxArendal, November 2022), www.ted.com/talks/peder_tellefsdal_how_to_seek_forgiveness_when_relationships_are_on_the_line, accessed December 19, 2025

12 J Levenson, "The surprising ways space technology can save our oceans"

(TEDxFoggyBottom, November 29, 2025), www.youtube.com/watch?v=3mJwL1xZ2Sw, accessed December 19, 2025

13 M Shoreman, "How to keep going when life seems impossible" (TEDxWesternU, May 2, 2024), www.youtube.com/watch?v=rjgnbrGq30I, accessed December 19, 2025

14 Generation180, "Your influence matters: Peer influence and electric vehicle adoption" (Generation180, October 26, 2023), https://generation180.org/resource/your-influence-matters-peer-influence-and-electric-vehicle-adoption, accessed January 1, 2026

15 T Webster, "The best place to start your message" (LinkedIn, June 8, 2023), www.linkedin.com/pulse/best-place-start-your-message-tamsen-webster-1e, accessed December 18, 2025.

16 Y Saad, "How to make sense of your negative thoughts" (TEDxOltrarno, April 18, 2025), www.youtube.com/watch?v=HVAZnIxtuBY, accessed December 19, 2025

17 M Rutherford, *Perfectly Hidden Depression: How to break free from perfectionism, find self-acceptance, and live a happier life* (New Harbinger, 2019)

18 M Rutherford, "How to recognize perfectly hidden depression" (TEDxBocaRaton, June 29, 2023), https://drmargaretrutherford.com/tedx-talk, accessed December 19, 2025

19 N Fung, "How to support someone without having the solution" (TEDxUofW, August 12, 2024), www.youtube.com/watch?v=EbNAXpCnjTg, accessed December 19, 2025

20 And if it hadn't turned out that the company uses super-harsh chemicals that are damaging to the environment and dangerous to kids, we would have booked them. We hired a different company that uses all organic spraying and have enjoyed our new backyard ever since. The pitch worked. Just not the product.

21 USAFacts, "Is flying safer than driving?" (USAFacts, updated December 16, 2024), https://usafacts.org/articles/is-flying-safer-than-driving, accessed December 19, 2025

22 G Abramovich, "Redefining health through vitality: New insight into five years of loneliness trends" (Cigna Group Newsroom, 2025), https://newsroom.thecignagroup.com/vitality-research-new-insight-into-five-years-of-loneliness, accessed January 1, 2026

23 M. Aunos, "What we can learn from parents with disabilities" (TEDxWesternU, June 15, 2023), www.youtube.com/watch?v=XeYYVz_PH30, accessed February 16, 2026

24 Y Saad, "How to make sense of your negative thoughts"

25 S Weinschenk, "The power of the word 'because' to get people to do stuff," *Psychology Today* (October 15, 2013), www.psychologytoday.com/us/blog/brain-wise/201310/the-power-of-the-word-because-to-get-people-to-do-stuff, accessed December 19, 2025

26 J Haidt, *The Anxious Generation: How the great rewiring of childhood is causing an epidemic of mental illness* (Penguin, 2025)

27 J Epstein, "Giving voice to sibling sexual abuse" (TEDxBocaRaton, April 22, 2022), www.youtube.com/watch?v=0X5TvYrHxTA, accessed December 19, 2025

28 C Theil and C Dorchak, "How to be an activist who creates real change" (TEDxAlexanderPark, August 12, 2024), www.youtube.com/watch?v=uN9FXrrXjvo, accessed December 19, 2025

Publicly Available Talks

Aunos, Marjorie, "What we can learn from parents with disabilities" (TEDxWesternU, Junc 15, 2023), www.youtube.com/watch?v=XeYYVz_PH30, accessed February 16, 2026

Blueweiss, Carole, "Your socks may hold the key to aging better" (TEDxBocaRaton, June 6, 2024), www.youtube.com/watch?v=6F6m9CGFnk0, accessed December 19, 2025

Coleman, Erika, "How to reduce stress without sacrificing success" (TEDxOneonta, October 4, 2025), https://youtu.be/9y1ZTgBClVI?si=zOe8_UaRu02PFtFo, accessed February 11, 2026

Epstein, Jane, "Giving voice to sibling sexual abuse" (TEDxBocaRaton, April 22, 2022), www.youtube.com/watch?v=0X5TvYrHxTA, accessed December 19, 2025

Fung, Nash, "How to support someone without having the solution" (TEDxUofW, August 12, 2024), www.youtube.com/watch?v=EbNAXpCnjTg, accessed December 19, 2025

Levenson, Jacob, "The surprising ways space technology can save our oceans" (TEDxFoggyBottom, November 29, 2025), www.youtube.com/watch?v=3mJwL1xZ2Sw, accessed December 19, 2025

Musa, Ndidi, "How to Live a Significant Life" (2026), https://www.youtube.com/watch?v=2dEW8wqQonE, accessed 16 March 2026

Rutherford, Margaret, "How to recognize perfectly hidden depression" (TEDxBocaRaton, June 29, 2023), https://drmargaretrutherford.com/tedx-talk, accessed December 19, 2025

Saad, Yasmine, "How to make sense of your negative thoughts" (TEDxOltrarno, April 18, 2025), www.youtube.com/watch?v=HVAZnIxtuBY, accessed December 19, 2025

Shoreman, Mike, "How to keep going when life seems impossible" (TEDxWesternU, May 2, 2024), www.youtube.com/watch?v=rjgnbrGq30I, accessed December 19, 2025

Tellefsdal, Peder, "How to seek forgiveness when relationships are on the line" (TEDxArendal, November 2022), www.ted.com/talks/peder_tellefsdal_how_to_seek_forgiveness_when_

relationships_are_on_the_line, accessed December 19, 2025

Theil, Carey and Dorchak, Christine, "How to be an activist who creates real change" (TEDxAlexanderPark, August 12, 2024), www.youtube.com/watch?v=uN9FXrrXjvo, accessed December 19, 202

Acknowledgments

I'd like to thank everyone who has ever hired me to speak, hired me to teach them how to speak, or listened to me talk about speaking. But since that list would be longer than this book, here are a few specific shout-outs.

Lindsey, for quietly providing me a stable foundation so I can comfortably take big risks. Your "treat yourself" attitude has led to me owning far too many guitars, but also to some of the most rewarding work I've ever done. Thank you for believing in me without qualification, through magic, speaking, consulting, and whatever's next.

Milo, for reminding me constantly that none of this work crap really matters. I'm a better person, and ironically a better professional, for it.

Dad, for showing me what's possible for an audience when an expert delivers a clear, compelling presentation on a complex topic. Sitting in the back of your lectures as a young child, I had no idea you were laying the subconscious foundation for my future career.

Mom, for your genuine enthusiasm about my work on message design, a field that strikes most as so boring it isn't worth asking about. I cherish our deep conversations on communication and appreciate your perspective from inside the corporate world (since, you know, I've never had a job).

Jill and Tom, for giving me a place to land when I was lost and directionless all those years ago. I owe my magic career to your generosity, without which the rest of this would have been impossible.

Grandma and Pa, although you're no longer with us, your unwavering and relentless support remains a constant presence in my life.

Francisco Mahfuz, for being the Costello to my Abbott. I've never had so much fun while doing such meaningful work. Your title may be "story specialist" but you've become so much more than that: confidante, thought partner, and a dear friend. Your comments and suggestions while writing this book were instrumental.

Ioana Jongsma, for challenging me with warmth and grace. You've changed my mind on topics no one else can. And while this book remains somewhat stubborn in terms of my core philosophy, it is far better than it would have been without your input and perspective.

Liwy Villaflores, for the lovely images in this book. But mostly for being an absolute rock star and my true right hand.

Tamsen Webster, because we all stand on the shoulders of giants. And while you graciously refer to me as a colleague, I still very much see you as a mentor. Our work has run parallel in some ways, but I am constantly bowled over by the quality of your work and the precision of your insights, which shapes how I think, write, and deliver.

Seth Godin, for showing me you don't have to choose between being both a world-class professional and a world-class human.

Michael Koch, for your consistent pursuit of excellence in teaching, proving it's possible to engage and delight even the most disinterested audience on difficult or even esoteric topics.

Erika Coleman, for graciously giving me permission to include your story and script as the primary example in this book. But also for being just an absolute blast to work with. It's an honor to help you ship your ideas into the world.

Jake Levenson, for also allowing me to tell the behind-the-scenes story of our work together in service of the reader. Your work is selfless, innovative, and deserves to be known.

All my clients who served as reader examples in this book, including Dr. Marjorie Aunos, Peder Tellefsdal, Dr. Margaret Rutherford, Dr. Yasmine Saad, Dr. Carole Blueweiss, Mike Shoreman, Carey Theil and Christine Dorchak, Jane Epstein, Dr. Heather Finley, Dr. Ndidi Musa, and Nash Fung.

And of course to our hundreds of clients who were not featured in this book but whose work is important and we are so proud to be associated with.

Finally, two special mentions:

First, Heatherlyn Schoeppich. You showed up for years while I struggled to deal with a devastating situation in my personal life. Even when I didn't respond. Even when I couldn't engage. Even when everyone else had moved on. You were there the whole time, and I am forever grateful.

Adam. I miss you every second of every day. My best friend. My lifelong thought partner. The best human and most creative mind I have ever known. Your memory alone inspires me to do better, to be better. On to the next project.

The Author

Brian Miller is a former magician turned international keynote speaker, author, and messaging consultant. His TEDx talk on human connection has been viewed over 3.6 million times, launching a speaking career that has taken him to hundreds of stages across five continents.

Today, Brian is the founder and principal consultant at Clarity Up, a boutique messaging firm that teaches experts how to explain their big ideas to the rest of us. His team has served hundreds of individuals across over twenty industries, helping industry leaders, scientists, academics, and advocates craft presentations that move audiences to action.

Brian's work has earned multiple honors, including the 2025 Cicero Speechwriting Award and two 2025 Anthem Awards for social impact. He has been a trusted adviser to leaders at nonprofits, healthcare organizations, unicorn tech companies, and a government agency—as well as individual advocates, activists, and thought leaders.

Brian is also the author of *Three New People*, which explores the art of making meaningful connections with strangers. *Publishers Weekly* raved, "Miller brilliantly outlines a system for deepening relationships."

Before his career in speaking and consulting, Brian spent nearly a decade as a professional magician, performing at corporate events and private engagements while developing the audience-first instincts that now inform his approach to message design. He holds that the principles of great magic—clarity, structure, and story—are the same principles that make ideas stick.

Brian lives in Virginia with his wife, Lindsey, and their son, Milo. Brian believes everything can be said clearly—and he's on a mission to restore humanity's faith in experts.

https://clarityupconsulting.com

https://brianmillerspeaks.com

https://linkedin.com/in/brianmillerspeaks

@brianmillerspeaks

www.ingramcontent.com/pod-product-compliance
Lightning Source LLC
LaVergne TN
LVHW010605100826
845148LV00014B/2853

9781781339800